10 Minute Guide to
Lotus® 1-2-3® for Windows™

Peter Aitken

A Division of Macmillan Computer Publishing
11711 North College, Carmel, Indiana 46032 USA

International Standard Book Number: 0-672-30082-6
Library of Congress Catalog Card Number: 91-62360

Publisher: *Richard K. Swadley*
Publishing Manager and Acquisitions Editor: *Marie Butler-Knight*
Managing Editor: *Marjorie Hopper*
Development Editor: *Lisa Bucki*
Technical Editor: *C. Herbert Feltner*
Manuscript Editor: *Faithe Wempen*
Cover Designer: *Dan Armstrong*
Designer: *Scott Cook and reVisions Plus, Inc.*
Indexer: *Jeanne Clark*
Production Assistance: *Scott Boucher, Martin Coleman, Bob LaRoche, Sarah Leatherman, Laurie Lee, Julie Pavey, Dennis Sheehan*

Screen reproductions in this book were created by means of the program Collage Plus from Inner Media, Inc., Hollis, NH.

Printed in the United States of America

Trademarks

Contents

Introduction

Lotus 1-2-3 is one of the most popular applications programs ever, and the Microsoft Windows operating environment has taken the PC world by storm over the past couple of years. It was inevitable that the two should come together, and now they have—as Lotus 1-2-3 for Windows.

If you're one of the many people just starting with 1-2-3 for Windows, you're probably looking for a quick method of learning the most important features of the program. You want to get up and running quickly, and start using 1-2-3 for Windows productively. You don't have the time to sit down and read the program documentation or a 600-page book. You can, however, find 10 minutes here and there in your busy schedule.

Welcome to the 10 Minute Guide to 1-2-3 for Windows! This book is, I believe, just what you need. It teaches you the basics of 1-2-3 for Windows in a series of short lessons that can each be completed in 10 minutes or less. Because each lesson is self-contained, you can start and stop as your schedule allows. This and other features of the 10 Minute Guide to 1-2-3 for Windows make it ideal for anyone who:

- Has a limited amount of time to spend learning the program.

- Is overwhelmed by the complexity of 1-2-3 for Windows.

- Wants a clear, concise guide to the program's most important features.

- Needs to determine if 1-2-3 for Windows will meet his or her needs.

What Is the 10 Minute Guide?

The 10 Minute Guide is a new approach to computer books. Rather than trying to cover every detail of a program, the Guide shows you how to use just those features that are essential. Plain English is used to explain things; technical jargon and "computerese" are avoided.

The following icons are used to help you find information quickly:

Timesaver Tip icons offer shortcuts and hints for using the program effectively.

Plain English icons define new terms.

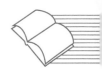

Panic Button icons appear where new users often run into trouble.

In addition, several conventions used in the book help clarify the information presented:

- Numbered steps are given, providing specific instructions for frequently-needed procedures.

- Any keystrokes you enter are printed in color to make them easy to locate.

- Menu names, dialog box titles, and commands are printed with the first letter capitalized for easy recognition.

The inside front cover presents instructions for Installing 1-2-3 for Windows, and the inside back cover presents information on SmartIcons, one of 1-2-3 for Windows' innovative features.

The 10 Minute Guide to 1-2-3 for Windows contains 22 lessons. Most readers will want to work through the lessons in order. After reading the first 5 lessons, however, you can jump around if you need to find specific information quickly. Once you've finished this book, you may want a more detailed book on 1-2-3 for Windows. Here are some suggestions, also published by SAMS, that I recommend:

The First Book of 1-2-3 for Windows

10 Minute Guide to Windows 3

10 Minute Guide to MS-DOS

The First Book of MS-DOS

The Best Book of MS-DOS

Lessons

Starting 1-2-3 for Windows

In this lesson, you'll learn how to start 1-2-3 for Windows, how to use a mouse, and what the major parts of the 1-2-3 screen are.

Starting 1-2-3

To start 1-2-3 for Windows, it must be installed on your system. (Refer to the inside front cover of this book for installation instructions.) Start 1-2-3 for Windows from the Windows Program Manager screen. After you install 1-2-3, the Program manager screen will include a Lotus Applications window. (See Figure 1.1.) Start 1-2-3 for Windows by selecting the 1-2-3 icon in the Lotus Applications window, as follows:

1. If the Program Manager screen is not visible, press Alt-Esc one or more times to display it. (Press and hold the Alt key, press the Esc key, then release both keys.)

2. If necessary, press Ctrl-F6 one or more times to bring the Lotus Applications window to the top of the Program Manager screen (as it is in Figure 1.1).

3. *With the mouse*, position the mouse pointer on the 1-2-3 for Windows icon, then rapidly press and release

1

the left mouse button twice. OR, *with the keyboard*, use the arrow keys to move the highlight to the 1-2-3 for Windows icon, then press Enter.

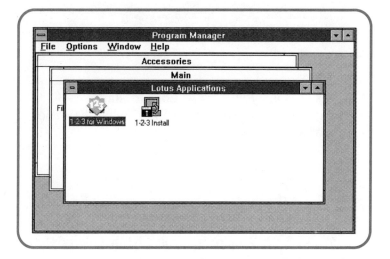

Figure 1.1 The Windows Program Manager Screen.

 Icon An *icon* is a small graphic symbol that represents a program or screen window.

The 1-2-3 Screen

When it starts, 1-2-3 for Windows displays its opening logo for a few seconds, then displays the 1-2-3 screen with a blank worksheet window. (See Figure 1.2.) This figure identifies the important components of the 1-2-3 screen as follows:

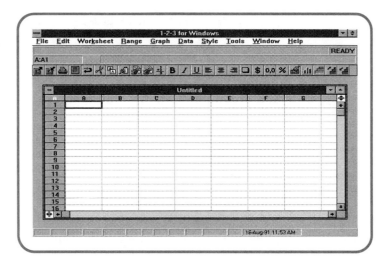

Figure 1.2 The 1-2-3 screen with a blank worksheet.

- The *title bar* shows the name of the program being run.

- The *menu bar* displays program commands.

- The *indicator line* displays information about cells.

- The *control line* is used to display and enter data.

- The *worksheet window* displays a worksheet. The worksheet in Figure 1.2 is blank (contains no data).

- The *work area* is where 1-2-3 displays worksheet and graph windows.

- The *cell pointer* is a rectangle that indicates the current worksheet cell.

- The *Icon Palette* displays *SmartIcons* for performing common tasks with a mouse.

• The *status line* displays information about 1-2-3's status.

Using a Mouse

1-2-3 for Windows makes extensive use of a mouse. You can use 1-2-3 for Windows without a mouse, but having one makes most operations much faster and easier. Most procedures described in this book assume you'll be using a mouse, but keyboard instructions are included where appropriate.

The *mouse pointer* is an arrow or other symbol that moves on the screen as you move the mouse on your desk. The shape of the mouse pointer varies depending on the current operation. For now you need to know these two:

• An *arrow* is the default pointer shape, and means that you can perform normal operations.

• An *hourglass* means that 1-2-3 is busy and you must wait. The hourglass pointer moves in response to the mouse, but you cannot take any action or enter any commands while the hourglass pointer appears.

Here are the most important mouse actions:

Point	Position the mouse pointer at a specific screen location.
Click	Press and release the left button.
Double-click	Quickly press and release the left mouse button twice.
Drag	Move the mouse while holding the left button down.

Lesson 2
Controlling Screen Windows

In this lesson, you will learn how to control the screen windows that 1-2-3 for Windows uses to display worksheet data and graphs.

The Parts of a Window

Like other programs that run under Microsoft Windows, 1-2-3 uses screen windows to display data and other program information. 1-2-3's work area can display one or more windows at once. All windows are the same, in terms of their components and what you can do with them. The components of a window are illustrated in Figure 2.1.

The Window Control Menu

Every window has its own *Window Control menu*. If you're using the keyboard, you use the commands on the Window Control menu to change the size and position of the window. If you're using the mouse, you can perform these tasks with or without the menu (as will be explained in the following section). To display the Window Control menu, press Alt- – (Alt and the hyphen key) or click the Window Control menu box. Figure 2.2 shows the Window Control menu. Click again to return to Ready mode.

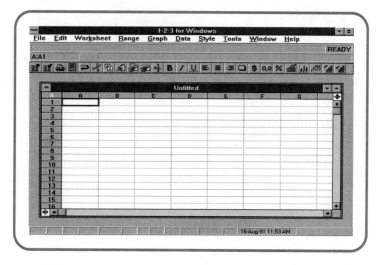

Figure 2.1 The components of a window.

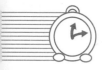

Entering keystroke combinations Special keystroke combinations that you must enter are printed separated by a hyphen. For example, Alt-F4 means to press and hold the Alt key, press the F4 key, then release both keys.

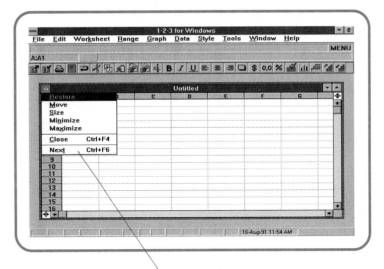

Figure 2.2 The Window Control menu.

Changing Window Size

When a window is first created, 1-2-3 for Windows displays it as a medium-sized window, occupying only a portion of the total work area. You can change a window to any size you desire. Following are the steps.

Using the Mouse:

1. Move the mouse pointer to any border or corner of the window. The pointer will change to a double-headed arrow.

2. Press and hold the left mouse button.

3. Drag the window outline to the desired size, and release the mouse button.

7

Using the Keyboard:

1. Press Alt- – to display the Window Control Menu.

2. Press S to select the Size command.

3. Use the arrow keys to move the window outline to the desired size.

4. Press Enter.

Maximizing and Minimizing a Window

You can also change a window's size with the Maximize and Minimize commands. A *maximized* window is the largest possible size, occupying the entire work area. A *minimized* window is reduced to an icon. The title of a minimized window is displayed under its icon. Figure 2.3 shows a maximized window. Following are quick instructions for maximizing and minimizing windows.

To maximize a window:

- *Using the mouse*, click the Maximize box.

- *Using the keyboard*, press Alt- –, then press X.

To minimize a window:

- *Using the mouse*, click the Minimize box.

- *Using the keyboard*, press Alt- –, then press N.

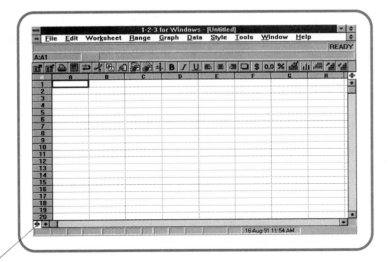

Figure 2.3 A maximized window occupies the entire work area.

Restoring a Window

A window that has been maximized or minimized can be *restored*, which means to return it to its initial size. In a maximized window, the Maximize box is replaced with the Restore box, which contains a double-headed arrow.

To restore a maximized window:

- *Using the mouse*, click the Restore box.

- *Using the keyboard*, press Alt- – and then press R.

To restore a minimized window:

- *Using the mouse*, double-click the icon.

• *Using the keyboard*, press Ctrl-F6 until the icon title is highlighted (if necessary). Then, press Alt- – followed by R.

Moving a Window

You can move any window that's not maximized to any position within the work area. When you have more than one window open, you can arrange their positions for best visibility. The following steps tell how to move a window.

Using the Mouse:

1. Point at the window's title bar.

2. Press and hold the left mouse button.

3. Drag the window outline to the desired position.

4. Release the mouse button.

Using the Keyboard:

1. Press Alt- – and then press M.

2. Use the arrow keys to move the window outline to the desired position.

3. Press Enter.

In this lesson, you learned how to control the screen windows that 1-2-3 for Windows uses to display worksheets. The next lesson will introduce two other important components of 1-2-3: menus and dialog boxes.

Lesson 3

Using Menus and Dialog Boxes

In this lesson, you'll learn how to use 1-2-3 for Windows' menus and dialog boxes.

Menu Structure

When working with 1-2-3 for Windows, you must use *commands* to instruct the program to carry out the desired tasks. Commands are often entered by means of *menus*. There are three types of menus in 1-2-3 for Windows:

The *main menu* is displayed in the *menu bar* on the second line of the screen.

A *pulldown menu* is associated with each choice on the main menu. When you choose a command on the main menu, its pulldown menu is displayed and a description of the highlighted comand appears in the title bar.

A *cascade menu* is associated with some (but not all) pulldown menu commands. The cascade menu is displayed when you choose the pulldown menu command.

These three types of menus are shown in Figure 3.1. When the menu system is active, the top line of the screen displays a brief description of the currently highlighted menu command. In Figure 3.1, the File Import From Text command is highlighted.

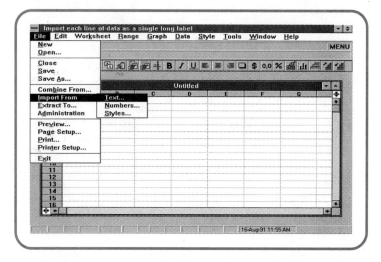

Figure 3.1 1-2-3 for Windows' three types of menus.

The pulldown and cascade menus use several conventions to provide additional information about the menu commands.

- A menu item is displayed in grayed text if that menu item is not currently available.

- A keystroke combination listed after a menu command, *accelerator keys*, is a way to execute the menu command directly without using the menu system.

- Ellipses following a menu command indicate that the menu command leads to a dialog box.

- An arrowhead following a pulldown menu command indicates that the command leads to a cascade menu.

- An underlined letter in a menu command denotes the key that can be pressed to select the menu command when the menu is displayed.

- The moveable menu pointer indicates the command that will be executed by pressing Enter.

Using accelerator keys You'll save time if you learn the accelerator keys for commands you use frequently.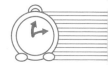

Making Menu Selections

You can select menu commands using the mouse, the keyboard, or the two used in combination.

To select a command from the main menu and display its pulldown menu:

- *Using the mouse*, click on the desired command.

- *Using the keyboard*, press Alt or F10 to activate the main menu. Then press the letter corresponding to the desired command (the underlined letter), or move the menu pointer to the desired command using the right and left arrow keys and press Enter.

To select a command from a pulldown or cascade menu:

- *Using the mouse*, click on the desired command.

13

- *Using the keyboard,* press the letter corresponding to the desired command (the underlined letter), or move the menu pointer to the desired command using the up and down arrow keys and press Enter.

When entering menu commands, you can cancel your most recent choice by pressing Esc. To cancel an entire command sequence, click anywhere outside the menu box.

Cancelling a command If you enter the wrong command, cancel it by pressing Esc one or more times.

For the remainder of this book, menu command sequences will be condensed. For example, if I say "select File Import From Text" it means to select File from the main menu, select Import From from the pulldown menu, and then select Text from the cascade menu.

Dialog Boxes

When 1-2-3 for Windows needs additional information to carry out a command, it displays a *dialog box.* Dialog boxes contain a number of components, illustrated in Figure 3.2. Many dialog boxes contain only some of these components.

A *dotted outline* indicates the current dialog box item.

The *title bar* gives the name of the dialog box, which is the command sequence used to display the dialog box.

A *text box* is used to enter and edit text information.

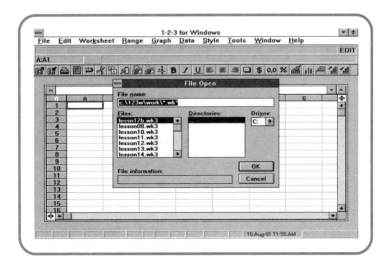

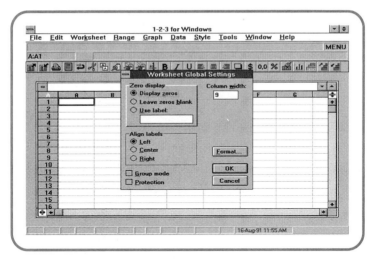

Figure 3.2 Components of a dialog box.

A *list box* displays a list of items from which you can choose. If the list is too big to display at one time, a *vertical scroll bar* lets you scroll up and down the list (more on scroll bars soon).

A *drop-down box* is similar to a list box, but displays only a single item unless it is opened.

An *information box* displays information about the item selected in the list box.

Check boxes turn options on (X displayed) or off (no X displayed). One or more check box options can be on at a time.

Option buttons also turn options on or off. Only one option button in a group may be on at a time.

The *command buttons* either confirm or cancel the dialog box.

Here are some techniques for controlling a dialog box using the keyboard:

To...	Do this...
Move forward and backward between items and groups of items	Press Tab and Shift-Tab
Move directly to a dialog box item	Press Alt-*letter* where *letter* is the letter under- lined in the item's name
Select an item within a group	Use the arrow keys
Select an item in a drop-down box	Use the Arrow, Home, End, PgUp, and PgDn keys to scroll among the items in the box (You cannot open a drop-down box with the keyboard)

Select an item within a list box	Use the Arrow, Home, End, PgUp, and PgDn keys
Toggle a check box or option button between on and off	Select it, then press the space bar
Cancel the dialog box without executing the command	Highlight the Cancel button and press Enter, or press Esc or Ctrl-Break
Confirm the dialog box and execute the command	Press Enter

And here are some methods of controlling a dialog box using the mouse:

To...	**Do this...**
Select an item or a list entry	Click it
Open a drop-down box	Click the adjacent arrow, and then select an item in the box by clicking it
Toggle a check box or option button between on and off	Click the box, button, or adjoining label
Cancel the dialog box without executing the command	Click Cancel

Confirm the dialog box and execute the command	Click OK

When a text box is selected, the editing position is indicated by a blinking vertical cursor. Any new text you type will be entered at the cursor position. You edit information in a text box as follows:

To...	Do this...
Move the cursor one character at a time	Press the left and right arrow keys
Move the cursor to the beginning or end of the text	Press Home or End
Highlight one character to the right or left of the cursor	Press Shift-left arrow or Shift-right arrow
Highlight all characters between the cursor and the beginning or end of the text	Press Shift-Home or Shift-End
Highlight characters with the mouse	Move the pointer to the first character, press and hold the left button, and drag the highlight over the desired characters

Delete all high-lighted characters or one character to the right of the cursor	Press Del
Delete the character to the left of the cursor	Press Backspace

In this lesson, you learned how to use 1-2-3 for Windows' menus and dialog boxes. In the next lesson, you'll be introduced to SmartIcons.

Lesson 4
Using SmartIcons

In this lesson, you'll learn how to use SmartIcons and to customize the Icon Palette.

What Is a SmartIcon?

A *SmartIcon* is a small graphic symbol on the 1-2-3 screen in the *Icon Palette*. Each SmartIcon is associated with an important worksheet command or task; when you click the SmartIcon the task or command is executed immediately. Figure 4.1 shows the Icon Palette with the default SmartIcons. (Your screen may show a different set of SmartIcons.) You must have a mouse to use SmartIcons.

Moving and Hiding the Icon Palette

The default Icon Palette position is near the top of the 1-2-3 screen, as shown in Figure 4.1. You can change the position of the Icon Palette, or hide it altogether, as follows:

* *Left*, *Right*, *Top*, or *Bottom* displays the Icon Palette at the indicated position on the 1-2-3 screen.

- The *Floating* choice places the Icon Palette in a window you can move to any screen location by dragging it with the mouse. You can resize the window by grabbing one of the borders with the mouse and dragging.

- If you select the *Hide palette* option box, the Icon Palette is not displayed.

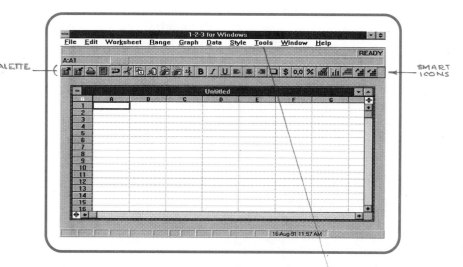

Figure 4.1 SmartIcons are displayed on the Icon Palette.

To move or hide the Icon Palette:

1. Select Tools SmartIcons to display the Tools SmartIcons dialog box.

2. In the dialog box, select the desired palette position, or select Hide palette, as previously described.

3. Select OK. The Icon Palette is displayed in the selected position, or hidden.

Adding and Removing Standard SmartIcons

A *Standard* SmartIcon is one whose function is predefined by 1-2-3. There are over 60 standard SmartIcons available. Only some of them are displayed on the Icon Palette at first. You can add, delete, and move SmartIcons to customize the Icon Palette to best suit your specific needs. To customize the Icon Palette, first select Tools SmartIcons to display the Tools SmartIcons dialog box. From this dialog box select Customize to display the Tools SmartIcons Customize dialog box (Figure 4.2).

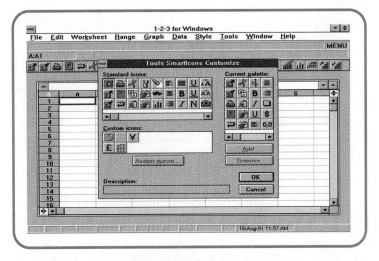

Figure 4.2 The Tools SmartIcons Customize dialog box.

Then, to add a SmartIcon at the end of the Icon Palette:

1. Select the desired SmartIcon from the Standard icons box. When a SmartIcon is selected, its description is displayed at the bottom of the dialog box.

2. Select Add.

Or, to add a SmartIcon at a specific location on the Icon Palette:

1. Under Current palette (which shows the SmartIcons currently on the Icon Palette), select the SmartIcon that you want immediately to the new SmartIcon's right.

2. Under Standard icons, select the icon to be added to the Icon Palette.

3. Select Add.

To remove an icon from the Icon Palette:

1. Under Current palette, select the SmartIcon to remove.

2. Select Remove.

Repeat these steps for adding or removing SmartIcons until the icon palette contains the SmartIcons you want to use. Select OK to redisplay the Tools SmartIcons dialog box, then select OK again. The Icon Palette is displayed with the new selection of SmartIcons.

In this lesson, you learned how to use SmartIcons. In the next lesson, you'll learn to move around in 1-2-3 for Windows.

Moving Around 1-2-3 for Windows

In this lesson, you'll learn the structure of a worksheet and how to move around 1-2-3 for Windows.

Worksheet Structure

1-2-3 for Windows keeps data in *worksheets*. A worksheet is like a page that is ruled into rows and columns. A worksheet contains 256 columns and 8192 rows. The columns are identified from left to right by letters A through Z, AA through AZ, BA through BZ, and so on up to IV. The rows are numbered top to bottom, 1 though 8192. Column letters and row numbers are shown in the *worksheet frame*, at the left and top edges of every worksheet window.

A 1-2-3 *worksheet file* is analogous to an entire book that contains as many as 256 pages. Each new worksheet file starts with a single worksheet. You can add additional worksheets, up to a total of 256. The worksheets in a worksheet file are labelled A: through IV:. The worksheet label is at the top left corner of the worksheet window. A worksheet window contains a single worksheet file.

Every cell in a worksheet file has a unique position, or address. A *cell address* specifies the cell's worksheet, column, and row position, as follows:

A:B2   Worksheet A, column B, row 2

D:F21   Worksheet D, column F, row 21

Every worksheet file has a single *current cell*, indicated by the cell pointer. The cell pointer is moveable (you'll see how soon), and the address of the current cell is displayed in the address box. Figure 5.1 illustrates cell addresses.

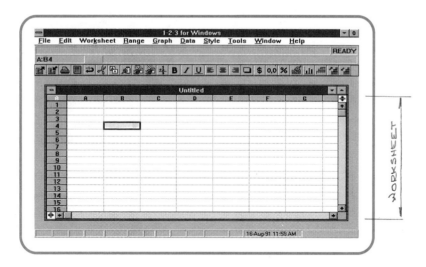

Figure 5.1 Cell addresses in a worksheet file.

Moving Around in a Worksheet File

A worksheet usually contains more information than can be viewed at once in the worksheet window. You can scroll the contents of a worksheet to bring different regions in view. You can use either the keyboard or the mouse to scroll. To scroll with the mouse you must use the *scroll bars*. The vertical scroll bar is used to scroll up and down, and the horizontal scroll bar is used to scroll left and right. The components of a scroll bar are shown in Figure 5.2.

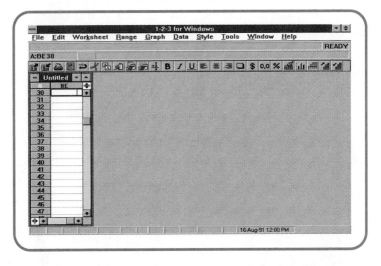

Figure 5.2 The components of a scroll bar.

Moving the cell pointer within a worksheet is easy using the mouse. Following are the techniques you should use.

To move the cell pointer...	Do this...
To a visible cell	Click the cell

Up or down one row	Click the up or down arrow on the vertical scroll bar
Left or right one column	Click the left or right arrow on the horizontal scroll bar
Up or down one page	Click the vertical scroll bar between the up or down arrow and the elevator box
Left or right one page	Click the horizontal scroll bar between the left or right arrow and the elevator box
To the top or bottom row	Drag the elevator box to the top or bottom of the vertical scroll bar
To the leftmost or rightmost column	Drag the elevator box to the left or right end of the horizontal scroll bar
To a variable location (vertical or horizontal)	Drag the elevator box to the desired position

It also is useful to know the keyboard techniques and shortcuts for moving around a worksheet, which follow.

To move the cell pointer...	**Press...**
Up or down one row	Up or down arrow key
Up or down one page	PgUp or PgDn
Right or left one column	Right or left arrow key
Right one page	Ctrl-right arrow or Tab

Left one page	Ctrl-left arrow or Shift-Tab
To cell A1	Home
To any cell	F5 (Goto), type the destination cell address in the dialog box, then press Enter

The End key can be used in conjunction with the navigation keys for rapid movement of the cell pointer. Press End followed by an arrow key, and the pointer moves in the indicated direction until it reaches the first boundary between an empty cell and a non-empty cell. If the row or column is empty, the pointer moves to the edge of the worksheet. Press End followed by Home to move to the lower right corner of the worksheet region that contains data.

Moving quickly to cell A1 To move the cell pointer to the top of the worksheet (cell A1), press Home.

Adding New Worksheets to a Worksheet File

A worksheet file starts off containing only a single worksheet, worksheet A:. For many applications a single worksheet is all you'll need. To use additional worksheets, you must add them to the file.

To insert an additional worksheet into a worksheet file:

1. Select Worksheet Insert.

2. In the dialog box, select the Sheet option button.

3. Select OK.

After these steps your worksheet file will contain two worksheets, A: and B:. Use the options in the dialog box to insert additional sheets.

Viewing Multiple Worksheets

Even if your worksheet file contains multiple worksheets, a worksheet window normally displays only one of them. This is the *current worksheet*, the one containing the cell pointer. You can display other worksheets by moving the cell pointer to them (as will be explained soon). You can also display three worksheets in a single window by selecting perspective view. Figure 5.3 shows a maximized worksheet window displaying three worksheets in perspective view.

To display multiple worksheets in perspective view:

1. Select Window Split.

2. In the dialog box select Perspective, then select OK.

3. To cancel perspective view and return to a single worksheet display, Select Window Split, then select Clear and OK.

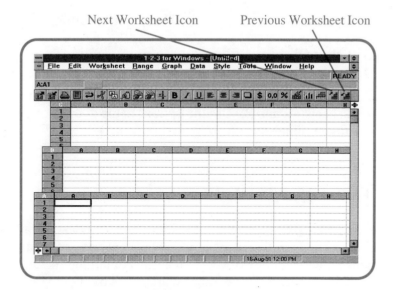

Figure 5.3 Perspective view lets you view three worksheets in a single window.

Navigating Between Worksheets

When your worksheet file contains more than one worksheet, you can move the cell pointer between worksheets using the keyboard, as follows.

Press...	To move the cell pointer...
Ctrl-Home	To cell A1 in worksheet A:
Ctrl-PgDn	To the previous worksheet (from B: to A:, for example)

Ctrl-PgUp	To the next worksheet (from A: to B:, for example)
End Ctrl-Home	To the cell in the lower right corner and the last worksheet in the file's data-containing area
End Ctrl-PgDn	Forward through worksheets, staying in the same row and column, to the first boundary between an empty and nonempty cell
End Ctrl-PgUp	Backward through worksheets, staying in the same row and column, to the first boundary between an empty and nonempty cell

Using the Mouse to Move Between Worksheets Figure 5.3 shows the two SmartIcons you can click on to move between different worksheets in a worksheet file.

In this lesson, you learned about worksheet structure, cell addresses, and how to move around 1-2-3 for Windows. The next lesson shows you how to enter and edit worksheet data.

Lesson 6
Entering Data

In this lesson, you'll learn about 1-2-3 for Windows' data types, and how to enter and edit worksheet data.

Data Types

A worksheet cell can hold two types of data: values and labels. A *value* is a number, while a *label* is any sequence of characters that is not a value. When you enter data into a worksheet cell, the first character entered tells 1-2-3 whether the entry is a value or a label. The following first characters signal a value entry:

A numeral (1, 2, 3, 4, 5, 6, 7, 8, 9, or 0)

(+ - . # @ or a currency symbol (for example, $)

All other characters signal a label entry. When you begin entering data, the 1-2-3 mode indicator at the top right of the screen shows VALUE or LABEL depending on the data type being entered.

Entering Values

Values are entered from the keyboard. To enter a value in a worksheet cell:

1. Move the cell pointer to the desired cell.

2. Type the desired value.

3. Confirm the entry by pressing Enter or by moving the cell pointer to another cell.

When you start typing an entry, characters you enter appear in the *contents box* of the control line. Figure 6.1 shows how the worksheet would appear after you move the cell pointer to cell B3 and type **123** but before you confirm the entry.

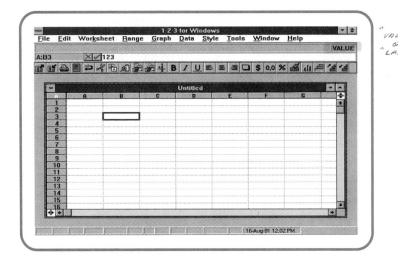

Figure 6.1 As you type in data, it appears in the contents box on the control line.

The parts of the control line are described as follows:

The *contents box* displays the current entry as it is being typed, or the contents of the current cell if no entry is being made.

The *address box* gives the address of the current cell.

The *Confirm* and *Cancel boxes* are used to confirm or cancel an entry with the mouse. They appear on the control line only during data entry.

When you confirm your entry, 1-2-3 enters it in the worksheet. If other data existed in the cell, it is replaced by the new entry. To confirm a data entry with the mouse, click another worksheet cell or click the Confirm box on the control line. To confirm an entry with the keyboard, press Enter or use any navigation key to move the cell pointer. Figure 6.2 shows the worksheet from Figure 6.1 after you confirm the data by pressing Enter or clicking the Confirm box.

Before confirming an entry, you can edit or cancel it. To cancel a data entry, click the Cancel box on the control line or press Esc. To edit a data entry, press Backspace to erase the mistake, then type replacement characters. After confirming an entry, you can edit the entry as described later in this chapter.

Entering Labels

1-2-3 for Windows stores labels with a *label prefix charac-ter* at the beginning. The label prefix character identifies the entry as a label, and also controls how it is displayed in the cell. The label prefix character is not displayed in the worksheet but is shown in the contents box when the cell pointer is on a label cell. There are three label prefix characters that determine how the label is displayed in the cell:

'   Left aligned in the cell

"   Right aligned in the cell

^   Centered in the cell

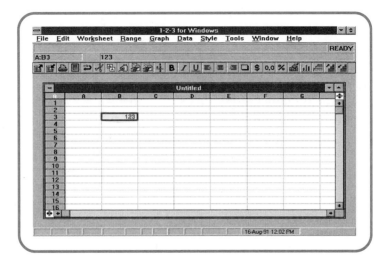

Figure 6.2 The data entry has been confirmed, and the value is now entered in the worksheet.

1-2-3 automatically inserts the label prefix character when you start typing a label entry. The default label prefix is left aligned ('). To enter a label that begins with a numeral or other numeric character, such as) or +, you must type in the label prefix character yourself. Otherwise, 1-2-3 will think it's a value entry.

A label can be up to 512 characters long, which means that you can enter a label that is wider than the cell. If the cells to the immediate right are empty, 1-2-3 will display the entire label, overlapping the empty cells to the right. If the cells to the right are occupied, 1-2-3 will display only part of the label. The entire label is, however, stored in the worksheet.

Entering a numeric label When entering a label that begins with a numeric character, remember to type a label prefix character first.

Entering Dates and Times

1-2-3 for Windows stores dates and times as special serial numbers, as follows:

Date	A value between 1 and 73050 representing the number of days since December 31, 1899
Time	A decimal fraction between 0 and 0.99999 representing the 24 hour day

Here are examples of date and time serial numbers:

Serial number	Date or time
1	January 1, 1900
73050	December 31, 2099
32978	April 15, 1990
0.0	12:00:00 AM
0.5	12:00:00 noon

Serial number	Date or time
0.25	6:00:00 AM
0.99999	11:59:59 PM

To enter a date or time, you enter it directly in a cell in one of the following formats:

Day-month-year	20-Jul-91
Day-month	20-Jul
Long international	7/20/91
Long AM/PM	11:30:45 PM
Short AM/PM	11:30 PM
Long 24 hour	23:30:45
Short 24 hour	23:30

1-2-3 for Windows will automatically recognize the entry as a date or time and convert it to a serial number. Date and time serial numbers are no different from other worksheet values, and will display as a number unless you change the cell's display format. Use the Range Format Date command, covered in Lesson 13, for this purpose.

Editing Data

To modify existing worksheet data, you use EDIT mode. Here are the steps to follow:

1. Move the cell pointer to the cell you want to edit.

2. To erase the cell, press Del. To replace it with new data, enter the new data as described above. To edit the cell contents, press F2 to enter EDIT mode.

3. You edit data in the contents box, using the following keys:

   To move the cursor one character at a time, press the left and right arrow keys.

   To move the cursor to the beginning or end of the text, press Home or End.

   To delete one character to the right of the cursor, press Del.

   To delete one character to the left of the cursor, press Backspace.

4. Type in new text.

5. To confirm your changes, press Enter or click the Confirm box. To cancel your changes, press Esc or click the Cancel box.

   In this lesson, you learned that 1-2-3 for Windows has two basic data types. You also learned how to enter data into a worksheet, and how to edit existing data. The next lesson shows you how to save and retieve files.

Lesson 7

Saving and Retrieving Worksheets and Exiting 1-2-3

In this lesson, you'll learn how to save your worksheets on disk and later retrieve them.

Saving a Worksheet

As you work in 1-2-3 for Windows, your worksheet data is kept in the computer's *random-access memory*, or *RAM*. RAM is temporary storage that loses its information when the system is turned off. To save your work permanently, you must save it to a file on a disk (either a diskette or a fixed disk). Each worksheet window is saved in a separate file on the disk.

To save a worksheet file under its existing name, use the File Save command. By *existing name* I mean the name displayed in the worksheet's title bar. The only exception to this is when the title bar displays Untitled, as the default worksheet does when you first start 1-2-3 for Windows. In this case, the File Save command automatically assigns a default file name of the form FILE*nnnn*.WK3 where *nnnn* is a sequential number.

You should avoid using the default file names. It's much better to assign your own names that describe the file's contents: SALES91, EXPENSES, MEDICAL, TAXES, and so on. 1-2-3 for Windows automatically adds the extension .WK3 to all files. To save a file under a new name that you specify, use the File Save As command, as follows.

1. Select File Save As.

2. In the dialog box (shown in Figure 7.1), select the File Name text box. You can edit the default name that is displayed there, or type in a new name. A file name consists of 1-8 characters.

3. Select OK. The file is saved to disk under the specified name. The file's new name now is displayed in the window's title bar.

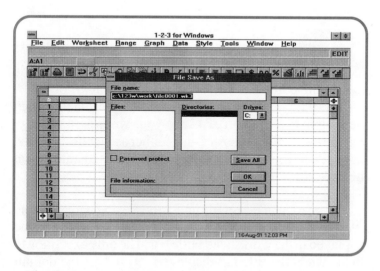

Figure 7.1 The File Save As dialog box.

Once a file has been assigned a descriptive name, you can save it quickly with the File Save command. When you select File Save, or click the File Save SmartIcon, the file is saved to disk under the name in its window title bar (except for untitled worksheets, as described above). If a file of the same name already exists, it is replaced with the new version.

Opening a Worksheet File

You can open, or retrieve, any worksheet file that has previously been saved to disk. When you retrieve a worksheet file, 1-2-3 opens a new window in the work area and displays the file. The worksheet title will remain the same unless you change it with the File Save As command.

To open an existing worksheet file on disk and read it into a new window, use the File Open command. In addition to WK3 files, you can open worksheet files created with Lotus 1-2-3 version 1.1 (WKS extension), 2.x (WK1 extension) and Symphony (WR1 and WRK extensions).

To open a worksheet file:

1. Select File Open, or click the File Open SmartIcon. The File Open dialog box is displayed (Figure 7.2). The File Name text box contains the name of the current disk, the current path, and the file name template. The Files list box contains a list of all files that match the template.

2. If necessary, use the Directories list box and the Drives drop-down box to select another drive and/or directory.

3. If you want to list files with an extension other than .WK3, edit the file name template.

41

4. Select the desired file name from the Files List box.

5. Select OK. 1-2-3 opens the file and displays it in a new window.

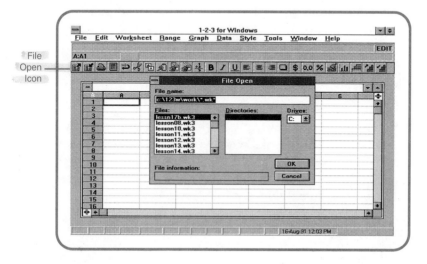

Figure 7.2 The File Open dialog box.

Opening a New Worksheet

To open a new, empty worksheet window, use the File New command. When you execute File New, 1-2-3 for Windows opens an empty worksheet window and assigns it a default name of the form FILE*nnnn*.WK3, as described previously. After entering data in the new worksheet, you can save it under a descriptive name using the File Save As command.

Closing a Worksheet

When you're done working on a particular worksheet file, you can close it to remove it from the work area. To close a file, select File Close. If the file has been modified since the last time you saved it, 1-2-3 will display a prompt asking you whether the file should be saved before closing. Unless you want to discard your most recent changes to the file, select Yes. The worksheet's window will be erased from the screen. The worksheet file will remain on disk, of course, and you can later open it when you need to work on it again.

Exiting 1-2-3 for Windows

When you're finished working with 1-2-3 for Windows, you need to exit the program to free up memory for working with other Windows applications, or in preparation for turning your computer off. To exit 1-2-3 for Windows, press Alt-F4 or select File Exit. If you have any unsaved data, 1-2-3 will ask you whether the file(s) should be saved. Then 1-2-3 for Windows will terminate.

In this lesson, you learned how to save and retrieve worksheet files, how to open a new file, how to close a file, and how to exit 1-2-3 for Windows. In the next lesson, you'll learn how to work with ranges.

Working with Ranges

In this lesson, you'll learn how to use ranges to manipulate worksheet data.

What Is a Range?

Many 1-2-3 for Windows commands affect the data in worksheet cells. For example, you can erase data, copy data, or move data to another location. Before you execute a command that affects worksheet cells, you must tell 1-2-3 which cells to operate on. You do this by defining the *current selection*, the cell or cells that your next command will affect. Unless you specify otherwise, the current selection is the single cell that the cell pointer is on.

Often, however, you will work with multi-cell selections, or ranges. A *range* is a rectangular region of cells that is defined by the cells at its upper left and lower right corner. For example, B3..C14 is a range containing cells B3, C3, B4, C4, and so on up to B14 and C14. A range can be any size from a single cell to an entire worksheet.

With most 1-2-3 for Windows commands, you can specify the range to be affected either before or after selecting the command. This book uses the method of specifying a range before the command is entered. When you select a range before choosing a command, the range remains selected after the command executes. This is useful when you need to use several commands on the same worksheet range. If you do not select a range before selecting a command that requires a range, you will be required to specify the range in the command's dialog box. See your 1-2-3 for Windows documentation for information on how to do this.

To specify a range with the mouse:

1. Move the mouse pointer to the upper left corner of the range.

2. Press and hold the left mouse button.

3. Drag the mouse pointer to the lower right corner of the range. As you drag, a highlighted rectangle expands to cover the range.

4. Release the mouse button.

To specify a range with the keyboard:

1. Use the navigation keys to move the cell pointer to one corner of the range.

2. Press F4.

3. Use the navigation keys to move the cell pointer to the diagonally opposite corner of the range. As you move the pointer, a highlighted rectangle expands to cover the range.

4. Press Enter.

When you have defined a multicell current selection, it is highlighted. For example, in Figure 8.1 the current selection is B2..D8.

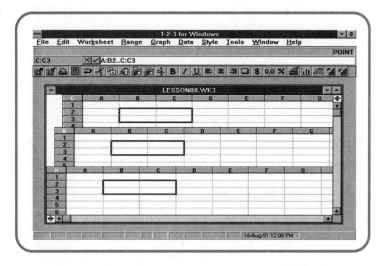

Figure 8.1 The current selection in the active window is highlighted.

If you highlight a range and then change your mind, you can cancel the selection by pressing Esc or clicking the left mouse button on a cell. After highlighting a range, you will often select a command that operates on the range. When you do this, the command's dialog box will automatically contain the range address in its Range text box. You can, if you wish, edit the text box to specify a different range.

Three-Dimensional Ranges

The ranges described so far have been two-dimensional, being contained entirely in a single worksheet. A *three-dimensional*, or 3-D, range spans two or more worksheets in a worksheet file. A 3-D range contains the same rows and columns in each worksheet. For example, a 3-D range could contain cells B2, B3, C2, and C3 in worksheets A, B, and C. This range would be indicated by the address A:B2..C:C3. This range is shown highlighted in perspective view in Figure 8.2. You do not have to be in perspective view to specify a 3-D range.

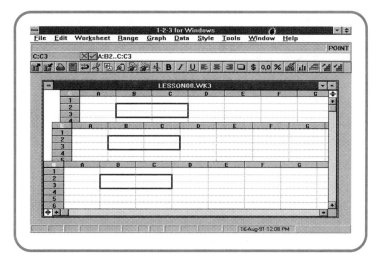

Figure 8.2 The 3-D range A:B2..C:C3 is highlighted.

You can specify a 3-D range anywhere a range is required, either before or after entering a command. You highlight a 3-D range with the keyboard.

To specify a 3-D range:

1. Move the cell pointer to the first or last worksheet that will be included in the range.

2. Using the techniques already described, highlight the desired row and column range in the worksheet.

47

3. Press Ctrl-PgUp or Ctrl-PgDn to expand the range to other worksheets, then press Enter.

Using Range Names

You'll sometimes define and use a range only once. Other ranges will be used over and over again. You can assign a name to a range, then refer to the range by its name rather than by its address. Range names you have assigned are saved with each worksheet file.

To assign a name to a range:

1. Specify (that is, highlight) the range to be named.

2. Select Range Name Create. The Range Name Create dialog box is displayed. Existing range names, if any, are displayed in the list box.

3. Type the desired range name into the Range Name text box. A range name may be up to 15 characters long.

4. Select OK to assign the name and close the dialog box.

For example, let's say you assigned the name SALES91 to the range A:A2..A:A20. You could then use the name SALES91 whenever you wanted to refer to that range. If you select a command that operates on a range and enter SALES91 in the dialog box's Range text box, the effect is the same as if you had highlighted the range A:A2..A:A20 before selecting the command. You also can use range names in 1-2-3 formulas, which are covered in Lessons 11 and 12.

Listing Assigned Range Names

To help jog your memory, you can create a table of all assigned range names and their associated addresses with the Range Name Paste Table command. The table is pasted into your worksheet and will overwrite existing data, so you must be sure to place it in an empty location. The table will contain two columns and one more row than there are defined range names in the current worksheet file.

To create a table of range names and addresses:

1. Move the cell pointer to the cell where you want the top left corner of the table placed.

2. Select Range Name Table Paste.

3. Select OK.

This lesson showed you how to define and name ranges in your worksheets. In the next lesson, you'll learn how to copy, move, and erase worksheet data.

Lesson 9
Copying, Moving, and Erasing Data

In this lesson, you'll learn how to copy, move, and erase worksheet data.

Cell Properties

Before getting to the main topic of this lesson, you need to know about cell properties. In addition to the data it contains, a worksheet cell can also have properties attached to it. *Cell properties* are settings that affect the appearance of the cell: font type and size, underlining, color, and so on. You'll learn the details of cell properties in Lesson 15. When you use 1-2-3's copy, move, or erase commands you can specify whether cell data, cell properties, or both will be affected.

Copying Data

When you copy data, the data is duplicated—it is present in both the original and new locations. Use 1-2-3 for Windows' Edit Quick Copy command to copy data and/or cell properties from one worksheet range to another range. Copying involves three steps:

5. Select OK. The data or cell properties are moved to TO range.

Erasing Data

You can erase data and/or cell properties from ranges of cells. You have two options when you want to erase a range of cells. Edit Clear erases all information—data, cell properties, and so on—from the range. Edit Clear Special lets you specify which information is to be erased. With Edit Clear Special, your options are:

Cell contents deletes the data in the cells but does not erase cell properties.

Number format resets all numeric formats in the range to the default format. Formats are set with the Range Format command (covered in Lesson 13). Cell data and other cell properties are not affected.

Style deletes all cell properties set with the Style command (covered in Lesson 15), such as font, borders, and shading. Cell data and other cell properties are not affected.

Graph deletes a graphic from the range. The graphic is not deleted from memory, and the data on which the graphic is based is not affected. You'll learn about graphs in Lessons 17 and 18.

To erase data, graphics, and/or cell properties from a worksheet range:

1. Specify the source of the data, called the FROM range.

2. Specify copy options, if desired. Two options are available:

    The *Styles Only* option copies only cell properties without copying cell data. The TO range receives the FROM range's cell properties while retaining its original data.

    The *Convert to values* option is relevant only if the FROM range contains formulas. This option causes the result of the formulas to be copied rather than the formulas themselves.

3. Specify the destination for the data, called the TO range. You need specify only the upper left corner of the TO range.

To copy data with Edit Quick Copy:

1. Highlight the FROM range.

2. Select Edit Quick Copy, or click the Edit Quick Copy SmartIcon on the Icon Palette. The Edit Quick Copy dialog box is displayed.

3. In the dialog box, select the To: text box, then specify the address of the cell in the upper left corner of the TO range.

4. Select the Styles Only and/or Convert to Values options, if desired.

5. Select OK. The data and/or cell properties is copied to the TO range.

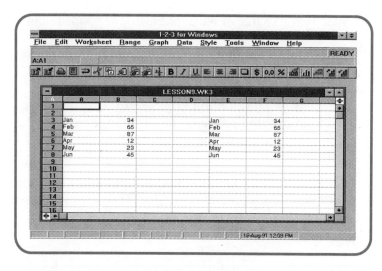

Figure 9.1 After a copy operation, the data exists in both the TO and FROM ranges.

You can specify a single cell TO range no matter how large the FROM range, and the entire FROM range will be copied with its upper left corner in the specified TO cell. For example, if the FROM range is A3..B8 and you specify E3 as the TO range, the effective TO range will be E3..F8. Under certain circumstances, you can use Edit Quick Copy to make multiple copies of data:

- If the FROM range is a single cell and the TO range is a multiple cell range, the data in the FROM cell is duplicated in each cell in the TO range.

- If the FROM range consists of several cells in one column, and the TO range spans more than one column, the FROM cells are duplicated in each column in the TO range.

Moving Data

Moving data moves data and/or cell properties from one location to another. Use 1-2-3's Edit Move Cells command to move data and/or cell properties from one worksheet range to another range in the same worksheet file. After executing an Edit Move Cells command, the data and cell properties exist in the new location and have been erased from the old location. Moving data involves three steps:

1. Specify the source of the data, called the FROM range.

2. Specify copy options, if desired. One option is available:

   The *Styles Only* option moves only cell properties without moving cell data. The TO range receives the FROM range's cell properties while retaining its original data; the FROM range reverts to the default cell properties while retaining its original data.

3. Specify the destination for the data, called the TO range. You need specify only the upper left corner of the TO range.

   To move data with Edit Move Cells:

1. Highlight the FROM range.

2. Select Edit Move Cells, or click the Edit Move Cells SmartIcon. The Edit Move Cells dialog box is displayed.

3. In the To: text box, enter the address of the cell in the upper left corner of the TO range.

4. Select the Styles Only option if desired.

1. Highlight the range to delete.

2. To delete all data, properties, and graphics in the range, select Edit Clear, press Del, or click the Edit Clear SmartIcon.

3. To delete selected information, select Edit Clear Special. The Edit Clear Special dialog box is displayed.

4. Select options in the dialog box depending on the specific information you want deleted from the range.

5. Select OK.

Deleting data To delete all data from a single cell, move the cell pointer to that cell and press Del.

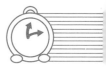

The Undo Command

Recovering deleted data The Edit Undo command can recover data that you accidentally erased.

If you mistakenly erase some valuable data, the Edit Undo command can usually save you. Many 1-2-3 commands or actions can be undone with this command. Generally speaking, you can undo any action or command that changes worksheet data or settings. Here are some examples:

* Deleting data

* Changing a cell entry

- Moving or copying data

- Changes in numeric format, font, and other cell properties

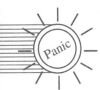

Using Undo Undo will work only if used immediately after the worksheet action you want to reverse.

And here are some things that *cannot* be undone:

- Changes to disk files

- A previous use of Undo

- Formula recalculation

- Printer activity

To undo your latest action, press Alt-Backspace, select Edit Undo, or click the Edit Undo SmartIcon.

In this lesson, you learned how to copy, move, and erase worksheet data, and how to use the Undo feature. The next lesson shows you how to insert and delete entire rows and columns.

Lesson 10

Inserting and Deleting Rows and Columns

In this lesson, you'll learn how to insert and delete entire rows and columns in your worksheet.

Inserting New Rows and Columns

You can insert one or more new, blank rows or columns in your worksheet. When you insert a row or column, existing data to the right of a new column or below a new row moves to make room for the new row or column. For example, if you position the cell pointer in column C and insert a new column, the worksheet will contain a new, empty column C; the original column C will now be D, the original D will be E, and so on. This is illustrated in Figures 10.1 and 10.2.

To insert a new row or column in a worksheet.

1. Move the cell pointer to any cell in the row or column where you want the new one inserted. For example, to insert a new column between the current columns A and B, put the pointer in any cell in column B.

2. Select Worksheet Insert. The Worksheet Insert dialog box is displayed.

3. Select Row or Column, then select OK.

4. The new row or column is inserted in the worksheet.

Figure 10.1 The original worksheet.

To insert two or more rows or columns at once, start by selecting a range that spans the desired number of columns. For example, to insert three new rows between row 2 and row 3, select any range that spans rows 2, 3, and 4 (for example A2..A4). Then select Worksheet Insert, select Row, and select OK. The original rows 2 and greater will be moved down three rows, and the three new rows will be inserted in rows 2, 3, and 4.

Cell referencing when inserting/deleting
When you insert or delete rows or columns from your worksheet, 1-2-3 automatically adjusts cell references in formulas.

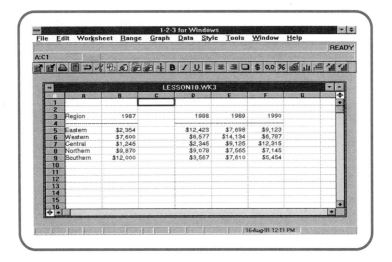

Figure 10.2 The worksheet after inserting a new column C.

Deleting Rows and Columns

You can delete entire rows and columns from your worksheet. When you do so, the data in the deleted area is gone, and rows below the deleted row move up, or columns to the right of the deleted column move left, to fill the space. For example, if you delete column C, the original column D will now be column C, column E will now be column D, and so on. This is illustrated in Figures 10.3 and 10.4.

To delete one or more columns or rows:

1. Highlight a range that includes at least one cell in each row or column to be deleted.

2. Select Worksheet Delete, then in the dialog box select Row or Column.

3. Select OK. The specified rows or columns are deleted.

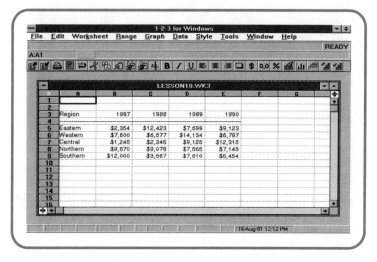

Figure 10.3 The original worksheet.

Undoing a row or column deletion If you make a mistake and delete the wrong rows or columns, you can get them back with Edit Undo.

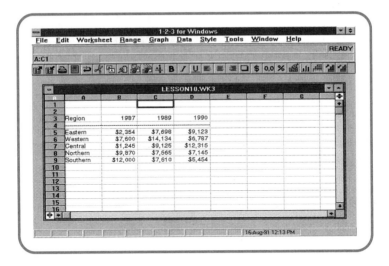

Figure 10.4 After deleting column C.

In this lesson, you learned how to insert and delete worksheet columns and rows. The next lesson shows you how to use formulas in your worksheets.

Writing Formulas

In this lesson, you'll learn how to use formulas in your worksheets.

What Is a Formula?

You have learned that a worksheet cell can contain either a value or a label. A cell can also contain a formula. This is one of 1-2-3 for Windows' most powerful features. A *formula* is a mathematical equation that performs a calculation based on data in a worksheet. Using formulas, your worksheets can be more than lists of numbers, and can do things such as:

- Summing groups of numbers

- Calculating averages

- Performing financial analyses

A formula can contain values and can also refer to values in other worksheet cells. Whenever data in the worksheet changes, formulas are automatically recalculated, keeping the worksheet up-to-date. A cell that contains a formula displays the result of the formula, not the formula itself. Let's look at some simple formulas:

If you enter:	The cell displays:
20/4	**5** (20 divided by 4)
+B3	The contents of cell B3
+B1+B2+B3	The sum of the values in cells B1, B2, and B3
+Total	The contents of the cell that has been assigned the range name "Total"
+<<SALES91>>A10	The value in cell A10 in the worksheet file SALES91.WK3

Looking at these examples, you'll note that to refer to the contents of another worksheet cell, a formula must include the cell's address or its assigned range name.

Entering a Formula

You enter a formula into a cell like any other entry. A formula must begin with a number, a left parenthesis, a cell reference preceded by a plus or minus sign, or the name of an @function. (These are 1-2-3 for Windows' built-in formulas, discussed in the next lesson.) In the cell, 1-2-3 displays the formula result, but the formula is displayed in the contents box when the cell pointer is on the cell (see Figure 11.1). In this worksheet, cell B7 contains the formula **+B2+B3+B4+B5+B6**, calculating the sum of the values in cells B2..B6. The worksheet displays the formula result, while the contents box displays the formula (when the cell pointer is on cell B7).

The formula
appears here . . .

. . . and the
results here

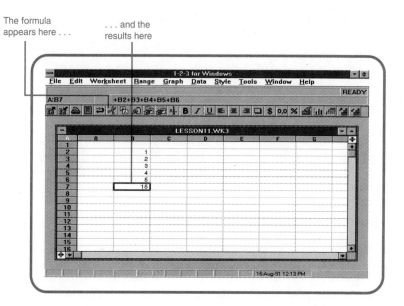

Figure 11.1 The worksheet displays the result of a formula, but the contents box displays the formula itself.

Formula Operators and Operator Precedence

An *operator* is a symbol that instructs 1-2-3 to perform a certain operation in a formula. 1-2-3's operators have a precedence that determines the order in which they are performed. 1-2-3 can use the five standard mathematical operators to perform numeric calculations in formulas:

+	addition
–	subtraction

*	multiplication
/	division
^	exponentiation

When a numeric formula contains more than one operator, 1-2-3 performs the operations in a particular order, or *precedence*. Operators with lower precedence numbers are performed first. The precedence of operators is:

Precedence	Operator(s)
1	^
2	* /
3	+ −

Operators with the same precedence are performed in left-to-right order. You can use parentheses to modify the order in which calculations are performed. Operations enclosed within parentheses are always performed first. Here are two examples:

Formula	Result
+4+2*5	**14** (The * is performed first, giving 10, then the 4 is added).
(4+2)*5	**30** (The parentheses force the + to be performed first, giving 6. The 6 is then multiplied by 5).

Displaying Formulas

1-2-3 for Windows' default is to display formula results in worksheet cells. When developing a complex worksheet, it is sometimes useful to have the formulas themselves displayed in the worksheet. You can do this by applying the Text format to cells. You'll learn how to do this in Lesson 13. You can also print a worksheet's formulas. See Lesson 16 to learn how to do so.

ERR and Errors: If 1-2-3 cannot evaluate a formula, it displays ERR in the cell. When this happens, check the formula for errors. Common errors include leaving out a closing parentheses, or mistakenly inserting a comma.

Editing a Formula

You can edit a formula the same way you edit any other cell entry. Move the cell pointer to the cell and press F2 to enter EDIT mode. Details of the editing procedure were presented in Lesson 6.

Understanding Relative and Absolute Cell Addressing

To use formulas effectively you must understand the distinction between *relative* and *absolute* cell references. This is particularly true when you copy or move cells that contain formulas. By default, cell addresses are relative. A relative cell address does not refer to a fixed worksheet location, but to a location that is relative to the cell containing the formula.

An example will make this clearer. In cell A2, enter the formula **+A1**. Because +A1 is a relative cell reference, the formula's meaning is "the value in the cell immediately above this cell." If you use the Copy command to copy the formula to another cell in the same worksheet, it retains its relative meaning. If, for example, you copy it to cell D8, the formula is changed to **+D7**, retaining its original meaning: the value in the cell immediately above this cell.

At times, however, you want a cell reference in a formula to refer to a specific cell or range no matter where the formula is copied to. In this case you use an absolute reference. An absolute cell reference is denoted by a $ (dollar sign) before both the column letter and row number in the address (for example, **$A$1**). If you enter the formula +$A$1 in cell A2 then copy it to cell D8, the copied formula will still read **+$A$1**.

You can enter absolute references by simply including the $ in the appropriate places as you type or edit the formula. You can also use the F4 (Abs) key to have 1-2-3 automatically add the dollar signs for you. If entering a formula, type in the cell or range address, then stop. Press F4 to add the dollar signs, then continue entering the formula.

Using absolute references Before copying or moving cells that contain formulas, examine the formulas to see if absolute cell references are needed.

In this lesson, you learned how to use formulas in your worksheets to perform calculations. The next lesson covers 1-2-3 for Windows' built-in formulas.

Lesson 12
Using 1-2-3 for Windows' Built-In Formulas

In this lesson you'll be introduced to 1-2-3 for Windows' built-in formulas, the @functions.

What Is an @function?

The 1-2-3 for Windows program includes an array of built-in formulas that are called *@functions* ("at" functions). You can use @functions in formulas in your worksheets, either alone or as part of complex calculations. Some @functions provide a quick way of performing commonly-needed calculations, such as summing a group of numbers. Other @functions let you do complex calculations, such as calculating depreciation, without you having to write the formulas yourself.

1-2-3 for Windows' @functions fall into eight categories:

Mathematical @functions perform mathematic calculation on values, such as calculating sums and averages.

Database @functions perform calculations on values in database tables (you'll learn about database tables in Lesson 20).

Financial @functions perform common financial calculations, such as loan payments.

Statistical @functions calculate statistical values, such as standard deviation and variance.

Logical @functions determine whether certain conditions in the worksheet are true or false.

Date and Time @functions are used to manipulate date and time serial numbers.

String @functions work with worksheet labels.

"Special" @functions that don't fall into one of the above categories.

1-2-3 for Windows has over 100 @functions. Obviously, we cannot cover them all in a 10 minute lesson! This section shows you the basics of using @functions. The Table of Functions near the back of this book also lists and describes more of the available @functions. You can also refer to the 1-2-3 for Windows documentation and Help system for details on specific functions.

Using @functions

An @function can be placed by itself in a cell, or it can be part of a formula. For example, to display the sum of the values in the range B1..B10, you would enter:

```
@sum(B1..B10)
```

If you wanted to display 10% of the sum of B1..B10, you would enter:

```
+0.1*@sum(B1..B10)
```

Each @function consists of the function name followed in most cases by parentheses. The function name always begins with the @ symbol. The parentheses enclose a list of one or more *arguments*. The arguments are the values or cell addresses that the function is to use in its calculations. A function's arguments can be values, cell addresses, range names, or even another @function. Here are some examples:

@function	Result
@sum(DATA)	The sum of all values in the range named DATA.
@pmt(5000, 0.10/12, 36)	The monthly payment on a $5000, 36 month loan at 10% annual interest.
@min(A:A1..A:A20)	The minimum value in the range A:A1..A:A20.
@avg(B2..B10)	The average of the values in the range B2..B10.
@sqrt(@sin(D1))	The square root of the sine of the value in cell D1.
@year(B10)	The year corresponding to the date serial number in cell B10.
@STD(<<DATA2>>A1..A20)	The standard deviation of the values in cells A1..A20 in the worksheet file DATA2.WK3.

@MAX(<<DATA2>> The maximum value in
SALES) the named range SALES
in the worksheet file
DATA2.WK3.

The following example demonstrates use of an @function, and shows you how to use POINT mode to specify a range address. The example assumes you want to display, in cell A5, the sum of the values in cells A1..A4.

1. Move the cell pointer to cell A5 and type @SUM(. (Stop after typing the open parenthesis.)

2. Use the up arrow key to move the cell pointer to cell A1.

3. Press the period key.

4. Use the down arrow key to move the cell pointer to cell A4. The highlight expands to cover A1..A4 and the range address is automatically entered into the @function in the contents line.

5. Type) (a close parenthesis). The cell pointer returns to cell A5, and the complete range address A1..A4 is entered in the @function in the contents line.

6. Press Enter. The @function is entered in cell A5, and displays its result.

You should spend some time becoming familiar with 1-2-3 for Windows' @functions. They can be great time-savers. And, you would not want to spend a lot of time writing a formula that duplicates an @function!

In this lesson, you learned about 1-2-3 for Windows' built-in formulas, the @functions. In the next lesson, you'll learn how to change your worksheet's number and label format.

Lesson 13

Changing Number and Label Format

In this lesson, you'll learn how to control the way numbers and labels are displayed in your worksheet.

Why Worry About Format?

The term *format* refers to the way that numbers and labels are displayed in worksheet cells. Format does not affect the worksheet data, only its appearance. Through careful selection of worksheet format, you can improve the readability of your worksheets.

The Numeric Display Formats

1-2-3 for Windows offers a wide variety of numeric display formats. When you start a new worksheet, all cells have the default numeric format. You can modify the format of cells in your worksheet with the Range Format command. First, however, you need to become familiar with the various formats that are available. This section describes the formats you'll use most often.

General format displays numbers with as many decimal places as needed, and displays negative numbers with a minus sign. General is the default format.

Value	Displayed As
106.99	106.99
−0.015	−0.015

Fixed format is essentially the same as General format, but the number of decimal places displayed (0-15) is specified by the user.

Value	Displayed As	Decimal Places Specified
106.99	107.0	1
106.99	106.9900	4

Currency format displays numbers with a currency symbol, thousands separators, and 0-15 user-specified decimal places. Negative numbers are displayed in parentheses. Comma format is identical to Currency Format except that no currency symbol is used.

Value	Displayed As Specified	Decimal Places
1000	$1,000	0
−50.95	($50.95)	2

Percent format displays numbers multiplied by 100, with a percent sign and 0-15 user-specified decimal places.

Value	Displayed As Specified	Decimal Places
0.15	15%	0
1.15	115.00%	2

Hidden format hides the data in the cell. The cell appears blank, but when the cell pointer is on the cell its data appears in the contents box. Use caution when applying Hidden format. Because the cell appears empty you may inadvertently type in new data, overwriting the old.

Text format displays the text of formulas rather than the formula's results. Values are displayed in General format. Use Text format to display formulas during worksheet debugging.

The *date and time formats* display date and time serial numbers in one of the available date or time formats. Here are examples of the five date formats:

Format	Example
Day-Month-Year	30-Jul-91
Day-Month	30-Jul
Month-Year	Jul-91
Long International Date	07/30/91
Short International Date	07/91

And the 4 time formats:

Format	Example
HH:MM:SS AM/PM	2:45:00 PM

2. Select Style Alignment. The Style Alignment dialog box is displayed.

3. Select Left, Right, or Center, then select OK. All labels in the range will be displayed with the specified alignment.

Changing the Default Display Format and Alignment

As mentioned earlier, 1-2-3 for Windows' defaults are to display numbers in General format and labels left-aligned. You can change these setting as follows:

1. Select Worksheet Global Settings. The Worksheet Global Settings dialog box is displayed.

2. To change the default label alignment, select Left, Center, or Right under Label Alignment.

3. To change the defalt numeric display format, select Format and then select the desired format from the dialog box that is displayed.

4. Select OK.

In this lesson, you learned how to control the format and alignment used to display numbers and labels in your worksheet. The next lesson shows you how to change the size of worksheet rows and columns.

HH:MM AM/PM	2:45 PM
Long International Time	14:45:00
Short International Time	14:45

Quickly identifying cell format When the cell pointer is on a cell that has been assigned a format by the user, the cell's format abbreviation is displayed at the left end of the indicator line.

Changing the Display Format

Each worksheet cell has its own numeric display format, which can be changed independently of all other worksheet cells. Changing display format has no effect on the data in the cell, only on how it is displayed. Initially, all cells have the default format—General. To change the format of a range of cells, use the Range Format command.

To change the numeric display format:

1. Highlight the range whose format you want to change.

2. Select Range Format. The Range Format dialog box is displayed (Figure 13.1).

3. Select the desired format from the list box.

4. If necessary, enter the desired number of decimal places in the Decimal places text box.

5. Select OK. Numbers in the range are displayed in the selected format.

Assigning formats with the Icon Palette The default Icon Palette has buttons for comma, currency, and percent format (all with 0 decimal places). To set these formats you can highlight the range and click the appropriate SmartIcon.

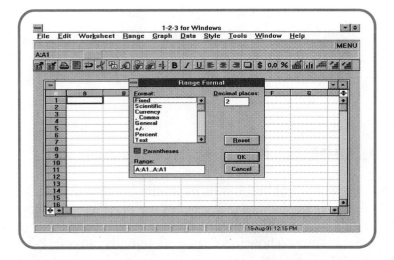

Figure 13.1 The Range Format dialog box.

To reset a range of cells to the default display format:

1. Select the range whose format you want to reset.

2. Select Range Format.

3. In the Range Format dialog box, select Reset. The range is reset to the default display format.

Changing Label Alignment

You learned in Lesson 5 that labels are stored preceded by a label prefix character ' " or ^. The label prefix character tells 1-2-3 that the cell contains a label, and also controls the way the label is aligned in the cell. The default alignment is left-aligned. You can change alignment with the Style Alignment command. Figure 13.2 shows examples of the three alignment options.

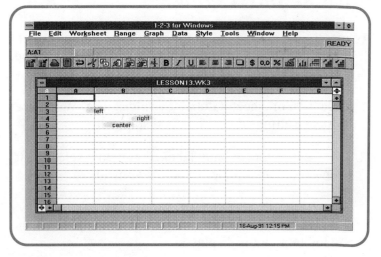

Figure 13.2 Examples of left-aligned, right-aligned, and centered labels.

To change label alignment:

1. Highlight the range of cells whose alignment you want to change. The range can include value cells—they will not be affected.

Lesson 14

Changing Column Width and Row Height

This lesson shows you how to control the height of rows and the width of columns in your worksheets.

Changing Column Width

The width of worksheet columns can affect the readability of your worksheets. Labels that are too wide for a column will overlap columns to the right if those cells are empty. Otherwise, only a portion of the label will be displayed. Also, certain numeric formats will display a row of asterisks if the column is too narrow. Conversely, a column that is wider than needed for its contents will waste space on the screen. Figure 14.1 shows a worksheet that uses the default width for all columns.

Every worksheet cell has a width that is determined by the width of the column it's in. You can adjust the width of each column in a worksheet. For example, Figure 14.2 shows a worksheet that uses different column widths.

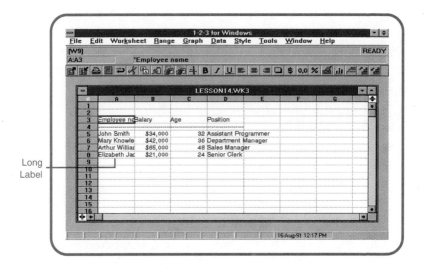

Long
Label

Figure 14.1 A worksheet with all columns at the default width.

The easiest way to change the width of a single column is with the mouse:

1. Move the mouse pointer into the worksheet frame that contains the column letters.

2. Grab the right border of the column being changed. The mouse pointer changes into a double-headed arrow.

3. Press and hold the mouse button, drag the column to the desired width, then release the mouse button.

To change multiple columns at once, for greater control, or if you don't have a mouse, you must use the Worksheet Column Width command.

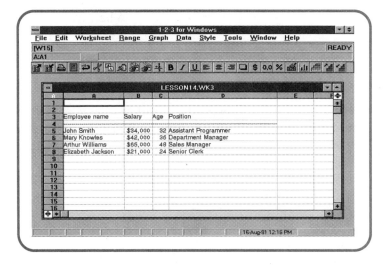

Figure 14.2 A worksheet with some different column widths.

To change the width of one or more columns:

1. Highlight a range that includes at least one cell in each column you want to adjust. For example, to change the width of columns A through C you could select the range A1..C1.

2. Select Worksheet Column Width. The Worksheet Column Width dialog box is displayed.

3. If it is not already selected, select the Select Set width to text box and enter the desired column width, in characters, into the text box. Or, if you want to reset the columns to the global column width, select Reset to global.

4. Select OK. The selected columns change to the new width.

Identifying the width setting When the cell pointer is in a column whose width has been changed, the width setting is displayed in the indicator line.

Column width is specified in terms of characters in the default font, which is Swiss 12 point. If you change a cell's font (as you will learn to do in Lesson 15), the actual number of characters that will display may be greater or less than the set column width, depending on the new font size.

All columns start with a global column width of 9 characters. You can change the global column width; the global width is used for all columns whose width has not been changed with Worksheet Column Width.

To change the global default column width:

1. Select Worksheet Global Settings.

2. In the Worksheet Global Settings dialog box, enter the desired width in the Column width text box.

3. Select OK, and all default width columns change to the new width.

Changing Row Height

1-2-3 for Windows' default is to set the height of each row to accommodate the largest font in that row. You can adjust row height manually as well. Row height is specified in *points*, with one point equal to 1/72 inch (This method is used because, as you'll see in the next lesson, font size is also measured in points).

To change the height of a single row, you can use the mouse:

1. Move the mouse pointer into the worksheet frame that contains the row numbers.

2. Grab the row border below the row being changed, and the mouse pointer changes to a double-headed arrow.

3. Press and hold the mouse button, drag the row to the desired height, and release the mouse button.

To change multiple rows at once, or if you don't have a mouse, you must use the Worksheet Row Height command:

1. Highlight a range that includes at least one cell in each row. For example, to change the height of rows 2 through 4 you could select the range A2..A4.

2. Select Worksheet Row Height. The Worksheet Row Height dialog box is displayed.

3a. If it is not already selected, select the Set height text box and enter the desired height.

3b. Select Reset height to return the rows to automatic.

4. Select OK, and the specified rows change to the new height.

In this lesson, you learned how to control the width and height of worksheet columns and rows. The next lesson shows you how to use fonts and borders to enhance the appearance of your worksheets.

Lesson 15
Using Fonts, Borders, and Shadows

This lesson shows you how to use fonts, borders, and shadows to enhance your worksheets.

Changing Font

Font The term *font* refers to the shape and size of the characters used to display and print data.

By using different fonts, you can increase the clarity and visual appeal of your worksheets and printouts. Some of the fonts available in 1-2-3 for Windows are shown in Figure 15.1. The exact fonts you have available will depend on your Windows installation and your printer. A 1-2-3 for Windows worksheet can display as many as 8 different fonts at one time.

Each font has a name that identifies the type style, such as Helvetica or Times. Each type style is usually available in several different sizes, which are measured in *points* (1 point equals 1/72 inch). You can add special attributes, such as boldface, italics, and underlining, to any font. The default font is 12 point Swiss.

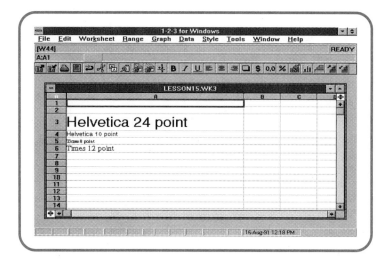

Figure 15.1 Some of 1-2-3 for Windows' available fonts.

To change the font used to display and print a range of cells:

1. Highlight the range whose font you want to change.

2. Select Style Font. The Style Font dialog box is displayed.

3. Select the desired font from the list box.

4. If desired, select the Bold, Italics, and/or Underline options. If you select Underline, choose an underline style from the drop-down box.

5. Select OK. The range is displayed in the selected font. Row heights are adjusted, if necessary, to accommodate larger fonts.

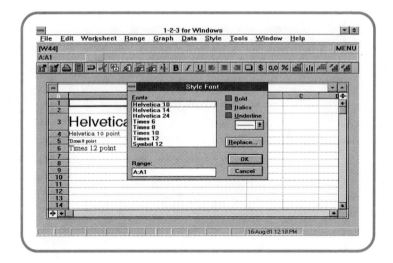

Figure 15.2 The Style Font dialog box.

Adding Borders and Drop Shadows

You can add borders and drop shadows to your worksheet cells. Borders are effective for setting different data areas off from one another, and drop shadows can be used to add emphasis to a worksheet or printed report. Figure 15.3 illustrates a worksheet with some borders and shadows added.

To add borders or a drop shadow to a worksheet range:

1. Select the range of cells.

2. Select Style Border to display the Style Border dialog box.

3. Select the locations to place borders in the range (see the list of border options which follows). Use the drop-down boxes to select the line style for each border.

4. Select Drop Shadow to place a drop shadow to the lower right of the range.

5. Select OK. The range is displayed with the selected borders and/or drop shadow. If you change your mind, select the Cancel command button to close the dialog box without adding a border and drop shadow to the selected range.

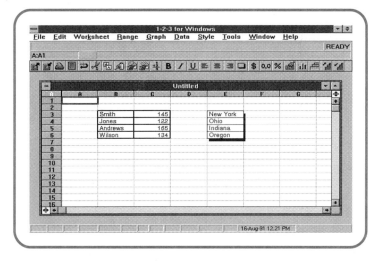

Figure 15.3 The range B3..C6 has a heavy single line applied to all edges; the range E3..E6 has a light single line applied as an outline, plus a drop shadow.

When adding borders to a range, you have the following placement options. For each placement option, you can select a thin single line, a thick single line, or a double line.

All Edges places a line around each cell in the range.

Top places a line at the top edge of each cell in the range.

Bottom places a line at the bottom edge of each cell in the range.

Left places a line at the left edge of each cell in the range.

Right places a line at the right edge of each cell in the range.

Outline places a border around the outer edge of the entire range.

In this lesson, you learned how to enhance your worksheets with fonts, borders, and drop shadows. In the next lesson, you'll learn how to print your worksheet.

Printing Your Worksheet

This lesson shows you how to create printouts of your worksheet data.

Printing with Default Settings

A worksheet printout can be as simple as a single column of numbers for your own reference, or a multipage, formatted document for distribution in your company. Creating a printout of your worksheet using the default print settings is very easy.

> **Printing a worksheet** To print, you must have installed a printer during the Windows installation procedure. The printer must be connected to your system, turned on, and on-line.

To print all or part of a worksheet using the default print settings:

1. Select the range to print.

2. Select File Print, or click the File Print SmartIcon. The File Print dialog box is displayed, as shown in Figure 16.1.

3. Select OK. The range is printed.

File Print
Icon

File
Preview
Icon

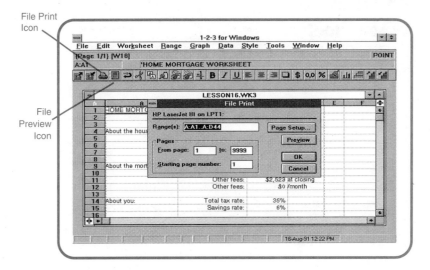

Figure 16.1 The File Print dialog box.

Selecting the entire worksheet To select the entire worksheet, press Home, then press F4, then press End Home.

Previewing a Print Job

The 1-2-3 screen shows a close approximation of what a printout will look like. Fonts, outlines, shading, and so on are similar in the printout to what you see in your worksheet. For an exact preview of the way the printout will look, you can use 1-2-3 for Windows' Print Preview feature.

To view a screen preview of a print job:

1. Select the range to preview.

2. Select File Preview, or click the File Preview SmartIcon. The File Preview dialog box is displayed.

3. Select OK. The first page of the printout is displayed in the Print Preview window (Figure 16.2).

4. Press Enter to view the next page, or press Esc to return to the worksheet.

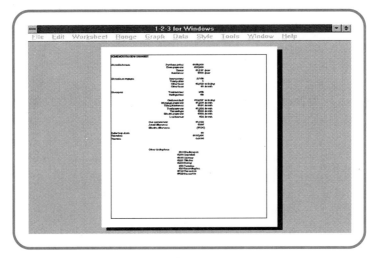

Figure 16.2 The Print Preview window with a page displayed.

Changing Page Setup

You use the *page setup* to change the way certain aspects of the printed page appear. Page setup is controlled from the Page Setup dialog box. You display this dialog box by selecting File Page Setup, or by clicking the Page Setup button in either the File Print or File Preview dialog box.

This part of the lesson covers the page setup features you'll use most often.

Setting Margins

A margin is the width of blank paper left between the printed area and the edge of the page. The default margins are 0.50 inch top, left, and right, 0.55 inch bottom. To change the margin, enter a new value in the corresponding text box in the Page Setup dialog box. To specify the margin in inches, follow the value with in. For centimeters or millimeters, follow the value with cm or mm.

Changing Compression

When you compress a printout, printed data is made smaller so more data fits per page. When you expand a printout, printed data is made larger so less data fits per page. There are three compression options:

> *None* disables compression. Data is printed at its normal full size (this is the default).

> *Automatically fit to page* compresses the print range, attempting to fit the entire print range on one page, if possible.

> *Manually size* lets you specify an exact compression/expansion factor. To compress the print range, enter a percentage factor between 15 and 99. To expand the print range, enter a percentage factor between 101 and 1000. For example, 50 compresses to half normal size, while 200 expands to double normal size.

Setting Page Orientation

There are two page orientation options:

Portrait (the default) prints the data with worksheet rows parallel to the short edge of the paper.

Landscape prints the data with worksheet rows parallel to the long edge of the paper. This mode is not available on all printers.

Printing wide worksheets Use landscape orientation and a compression factor less than 100 to fit wide worksheet ranges on single pages.

Print Options

In the Page Setup dialog box, you can select one or both of these options:

Show grid prints the worksheet grid (the vertical and horizontal lines between cells).

Show worksheet frame prints the worksheet frame (row numbers and column letters) on each page.

In this lesson, you learned how to create printouts of your worksheets. In the next lesson, you'll learn how to create a basic graph.

Lesson 17
Creating a
Basic Graph

In this lesson, you'll learn how to create a graph from your worksheet data.

Graph Basics

A *graph* is a visual representation of numerical data, and can be a very effective tool for summarizing numerical information. To use graphs effectively you must be familiar with the parts of a graph. Figure 17.1 shows a 1-2-3 for Windows graph with its components labelled. Every 1-2-3 for Windows graph contains some or all of these components.

Each graph is displayed in its own window. A graph window is similar to other windows in that it can be moved, resized, reduced to an icon, etc. The title bar of a graph window displays the graph's title. When a graph window is active, the menu bar displays the graph menu, and the Icon Palette changes to show SmartIcons for commonly-needed graph commands.

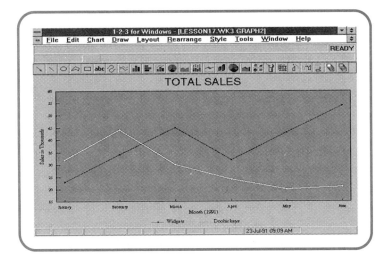

Figure 17.1 The components of a graph.

Graph Types

1-2-3 for Windows offers 11 different graph types. When creating a graph, you select the type depending on your data and the point you are trying to make. The table below summarizes the available types.

Line Graph	Plots each data value as a point or symbol, and connects the data points in each data series with a line. Suited for illustrating changes that occur over time.
Bar Graph	Displays numerical values as a set of vertical rectangular bars along the X axis. The height

of each bar is proportional to the corresponding value. Appropriate for comparing totals for several categories.

3-D Line Graph

Has the same basic structure as a line graph, but displays data in a three-dimensional perspective.

3-D Bar Graph

Identical to a bar graph except that each individual bar is given three dimensional perspective and appears solid.

Area Graph

A line graph in which data series are plotted "stacked" on each other, and the regions between plots are filled with a color or pattern. Use an area graph to illustrate trends over time when you want to show overall totals as well as the contribution of each series to the totals.

3-D Area Graph

An area graph displayed with a three dimensional perspective.

Pie Graph

Plots only a single Y-series, series A. The plot is a circle, with the entire circle representing the total of all values in the data series. The circle is divided into wedges; the size of each wedge represents the percentage that the corresponding value contributes toward the total.

3-D Pie Graph	Identical to a regular pie graph, but with added three-dimensional perspective.
XY Graph	Sometimes called a "scattergram." The only graph type that plots values on the X axis. Used to display the relationship, or correlation, between two or more sets of numerical values.
HLCO Graph	High-low-close-open. A specialized kind of graph used for stock market data.
Mixed Graph	Combines bar and line types in one graph. Data series A-C are plotted as bars, while series D-F are plotted as lines.

Creating a Graph

There are three steps involved in creating a graph:

1. Select the data to be graphed.

2. Specify the type of graph.

3. Enhance the graph with titles, legends, and other additions. This step is optional, and will be covered in the next lesson.

Selecting the data to be graphed means selecting one or more data series. A *data series* is a single row or column of values that appears as a plot in the graph. A graph contains between one and six Y-series, identified by the letters A through F. Values in each Y series are plotted against the graph's Y axis (or, in pie graphs, as wedges). A graph also contains one X-series, which consists of labels or values that are plotted on the graph's X axis.

Let's look at an example. Figure 17.2 shows a worksheet that contains some data to be graphed. We want to create a bar graph that shows the relative contribution of the Eastern and Western regions to sales for each of the 4 quarters. Here's how to do it.

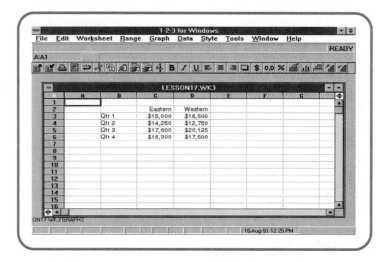

Figure 17.2 The worksheet data to be graphed.

1. From READY mode, select Graph New. In the Graph New dialog box, enter a name for the graph—for example, SALES.

2. Select OK. 1-2-3 displays an empty graph window. The title bar displays the graph name you assigned.

3. From the main menu select Chart Ranges. The Chart Ranges dialog box is displayed (Figure 17.3).

Moving around in dialog boxes using the keyboard You can move forward and backward between text boxes by pressing Tab and Shift-Tab.

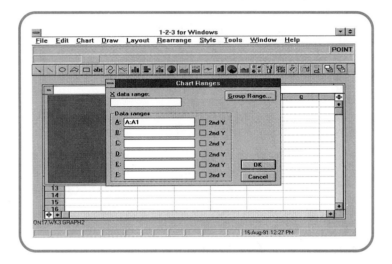

Figure 17.3 The Chart Ranges dialog box.

4. In the X Data Range text box, enter the range that contains the X data series. In our example, it is B3..B6.

5. In the text boxes under Data ranges enter the range C3..C6 for the A: range and D3..D6 for the B: range.

6. Select OK. 1-2-3 displays a line graph (the default type) in the graph window. Because we want a bar graph there's one more step necessary.

7. Select Chart Type to display the Chart Type dialog box. In the dialog box select Bar, then select OK. The window now displays a bar graph of the data (Figure 17.4).

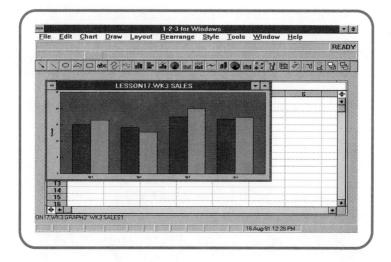

Figure 17.4 A bar graph of the sales data.

Automatic Graphs

In the preceding example, you manually specified the worksheet ranges to be graphed. If your worksheet data is organized properly, 1-2-3 can automatically assign ranges for you. All you need do is specify the rectangular range that contains the X and Y data series. For an automatic graph, data must be organized as follows:

- Y series data must be in adjacent columns, one column per series. You may have a maximum of 6 series.

- If the first column of the range contains labels, that column is used as the X series.

In the worksheet in Figure 17.2, for example, the range B3..D6 would be appropriate for an automatic graph. To create an automatic graph:

1. Highlight the range of data to be graphed.

2. Select Graph New, then enter the graph name in the Graph New dialog box.

3. Select OK. The automatic graph is displayed using 1-2-3's default type, Line.

Saving Graphs

You don't need to take any special action to save your graphs. All of the graphs you have defined are automatically saved with the worksheet file when you save it.

In this lesson, you learned the basics of creating a graph. The next lesson shows you how to enhance a graph.

Enhancing a Graph

In this lesson, you'll learn how to add enhancements to your graphs.

Graph Enhancements

The previous lesson showed you how to create a basic graph. Usually you will want to add enhancements to the graph. *Enhancements* consist of various additions and modifications to a graph that improve its appearance, clarity, and impact. This chapter introduces the most important graph enhancements. All graph enhancements are added from a graph window.

Adding Graph Titles

You can add a title and a subtitle to a 1-2-3 for Windows graph. The title is displayed centered above the graph, and the subtitle is displayed centered below the title. Figure 18.1 illustrates titles.

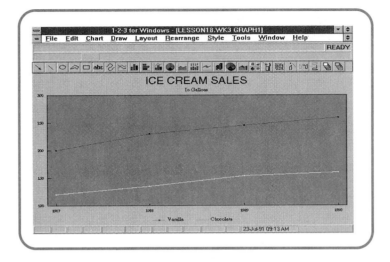

Figure 18.1 A graph with titles and a legend.

To add titles to a graph:

1. Select Chart Headings to display the Chart Headings dialog box.

2. In the Title and Subtitle text boxes, enter the desired text. To use a worksheet label as a title, enter the cell address or range name preceded by a backslash.

3. Select OK.

Adding a Legend

A *legend* is a key that identifies graph data ranges by the color, hatch pattern, or symbol used to plot them. Graphs that include more than one data range usually need a legend. The default is for a legend to be placed below the graph, as in Figure 18.1.

To add a legend to a graph:

1. Select Chart Legend to display the Chart Legend dialog box.

2. Enter the desired legend text in the text box for each data range. To use a worksheet label as a legend, enter the cell address or range name preceded by a backslash.

3. Select OK. The legend is added to the graph. 1-2-3 automatically puts the appropriate color, symbol, or hatch key adjacent to each legend label.

Adding Axis Titles

You can add a title to each axis on the graph to identify the data being illustrated. The X axis title is displayed below the X axis, and the Y axis title is displayed vertically next to the axis. You can enter a title from the keyboard, or use a label in a worksheet cell as a title. Figure 18.2 shows a graph with axis titles.

To add a title to a graph axis:

1. Select Chart Axis. From the cascade menu select the axis you are adding a label to (X or Y).

2. The Chart Axis dialog box is displayed. In the dialog box, select Options to display the Chart Axis Options dialog box.

3. In the Axis title text box, enter the desired axis label text. To use a worksheet label as an axis title, enter the cell address or range name preceded by a backslash.

4. Select OK twice.

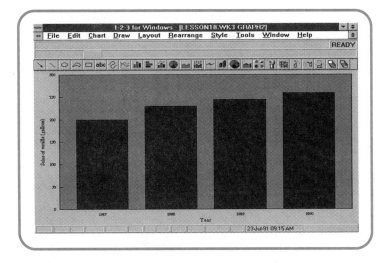

Figure 18.2 A graph with X and Y axis titles.

Controlling Borders and Grids

Graph borders are the lines displayed at the four edges of the data area (the lower and left borders are the X and Y axes). *Grid lines* are lines within the data area corresponding to axis tick marks. Grid lines are displayed perpendicular to their axis. Figure 18.3 shows a graph displayed with only left and bottom borders, and with grid lines on the Y axis. By default, graphs are displayed with all four borders and no grid lines.

To modify graph borders and grid lines:

1. Select Chart Borders/Grids to display the Chart Borders/Grids dialog box.

2. Under Borders, turn the check boxes on or off for left, right, top, and bottom borders.

3. Under Grid Lines, select one or more axes to have grid lines.

4. Select OK.

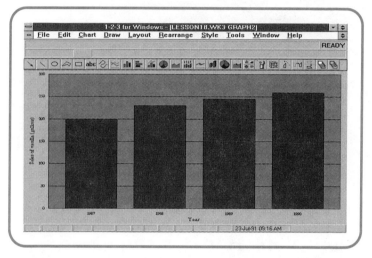

Figure 18.3 A graph with Y axis grid lines and left and bottom borders.

In this lesson, you learned how to add enhancements to your graphs. The next lesson shows you how to insert a graph in a worksheet, and print a graph.

Lesson 19
Inserting and Printing Graphs

In this lesson, you'll learn how to insert a graph in a worksheet, and how to print a graph.

Inserting a Graph in the Worksheet

Any graph you have created in 1-2-3 for Windows can be inserted in a worksheet. The graph will be displayed in the worksheet window, and will be printed if you print the worksheet range that contains the graph. By inserting graphs in worksheets, you can create sophisticated reports that include both data and graphs together. Figure 19.1 shows a worksheet with an inserted graph.

To insert a graph in the worksheet:

1. In the worksheet window, select the range to contain the graph.

2. Select Graph Add to Sheet. The Graph Add to Sheet dialog box is displayed.

3. In the dialog box, the list box lists the names of the available graphs. Select the graph to be added to the worksheet.

4. Select OK. The worksheet is displayed with the graph in the selected range.

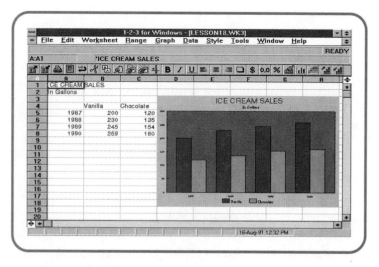

Figure 19.1 A worksheet with an inserted graph.

When you add a graph to a worksheet, it is scaled to fit in the range that you specified. Worksheet data in that range is not erased, but is hidden by the graph. If you return to the graph window and modify the graph, the changes will automatically be reflected in the worksheet graph when you next make the worksheet window active. If you change the data that the graph is based on, you must update the graph by selecting Graph Refresh from the worksheet window. This command updates all graphs in the current file.

To move the cell pointer to an inserted graph, select Graph Goto. A dialog box is displayed listing the names of all graphs that have been inserted in the worksheet. Select the desired graph, and the cell pointer is moved to the upper left cell in that graph's insert range.

Removing an Inserted Graph

To remove an inserted graph from the worksheet:

1. Highlight a range that includes the graph.

2. Select Edit Clear Special.

3. In the Edit Clear Special dialog box, select the Graph check box.

4. Select OK.

Printing a Graph

To print a graph, simply insert the graph in the worksheet, then follow the procedures you learned in Lesson 16 to print the worksheet. If the print range includes the range containing the graph, it will be printed. To print a graph by itself, without any worksheet data, specify the print range to include only the graph range.

In this lesson, you learned how to insert a graph in a worksheet, and how to print a graph. In the next lesson, you'll see how to create a 1-2-3 for Windows database.

Creating a Database

In this lesson, you'll learn how to create a database.

Database Fundamentals

A *database* is a collection of similar information with a uniform structure. Familiar database examples include mailing lists, merchandise inventories, and checkbook registers. In a hardware store's merchandise inventory database, for example, each entry, or item, has the same structure: part name, part number, cost, quantity on hand, etc.

Hammer	BN-654	$5.49	13
Wrench	HX-121	$8.85	8
Pliers	CV-413	$4.49	17

You need to know the following terms to understand 1-2-3 for Windows databases. A *record* is one complete database entry. In the preceding example, the information about each tool comprises one record. A *field* is an item of information contained in each record. In our example, there are 4 fields: part name, part number, cost, and quantity on hand.

The row and column structure of a 1-2-3 for Windows worksheet is ideal for a database. Each field has its own column, and each record has its own row. The top row of a 1-2-3 database contains the *field names*, which are unique names identifying the database fields. Field names must be labels.

The term *database table* refers to a rectangular range in a worksheet that contains information organized in this manner. A 1-2-3 for Windows database can consist of one or more database tables in different worksheets, but this lesson will limit discussion to single table databases. Figure 20.1 shows a small 1-2-3 for Windows database table.

Figure 20.1 A 1-2-3 for Windows database table.

There's only one restriction on the data that can be put in a database table. All the entries in a given field should be the same data type: values or labels. 1-2-3 for Windows will not prevent you from entering inconsistent data types in a database field, but unexpected results may occur later during certain database operations such as searching and sorting.

Creating a Database Table

It's a good idea to do some planning before you create a database table. You need to decide the following points:

- What information will the database table include? For example, does a mailing list need a separate field for "Country" or will it contain only domestic addresses?

- How will fields be ordered left-to-right in the database table?

- What field names will be used? You must use a unique name for each field, and they should be descriptive of the field's contents and also be as short as possible. For example, instead of "PART NUMBER" and "QUAN-TITY ON HAND" you could use "PNUM" and "QOH."

After you have made the above decisions, creating the database table is quite simple.

To create a new database table:

1. Select a worksheet region that has enough empty space to hold the table without interfering with other worksheet data. It's a good idea to devote an entire worksheet to your database table.

2. Enter the field names in the first row of the database table.

3. Enter the data for the first record in the second row of the table.

4. Enter data for additional records in the third and subsequent rows.

5. If desired, change formatting, label alignment, and column width to best display the data.

A database table cannot contain any blank rows. Individual records may contain one or more blank fields, as long as at least one field in the record contains data. To add data to an existing database table, simply move to the first blank row and begin entering the new data.

Data contained in a database table differs from other worksheet data only in that it is organized into a record/field structure. Otherwise it is no different from any other worksheet data. You can graph it, print it, edit it, copy it to other worksheets, use it in calculations, and so on. 1-2-3 for Windows also has some special capabilities designed specifically for use with database tables. The next two lessons deal with the most important of these capabilities.

In this lesson, you learned the fundamentals of creating a 1-2-3 for Windows database. The next lesson shows you how to sort the data in a database table.

Lesson 21
Sorting a Database

In this lesson, you'll learn how to sort a database table.

Sorting a Database

When working with a database table, one common task you'll need to perform is to sort your database records into a particular order. For example, you could sort a mailing list database into ZIP code order before printing mailing labels, or sort a customer database by "amount of sale" to find your best customers. 1-2-3 for Windows can sort a database table based on the contents on one or more fields. A field that is used to determine sort order is called a *sort key*.

You always use a *primary* sort key to order the records when sorting a database. Records in the database table are sorted according to the data in the primary sort key field. You also have the option of specifying a *secondary* sort key, which will be used to order the records when there is a tie in the primary sort key field. Additional *extra* sort keys may be specified to break ties in the secondary sort key field.

The sort order can be either *ascending* or *descending*. When you select ascending sort order, labels are sorted alphabetically A-Z and numbers are sorted smallest to largest. When you select descending order, labels are sorted Z-A and numbers are sorted largest to smallest.

To sort a database table:

1. Select the worksheet range that includes all of the database table records but *not* the table's field names.

2. Select Data Sort to display the Data Sort dialog box (Figure 21.1).

3. In the Primary key text box, specify the worksheet column that contains the primary key sort field. You can enter the address of any single cell in that column.

4. Select Ascending or Descending sort order for the primary key.

5. To use a secondary key, enter the address of any cell in the secondary key column in the Secondary key text box.

6. Select Ascending or Descending order for the secondary key.

7. If you need to use additional sort keys, select Extra keys and specify the field columns to use as extra keys in the dialog box.

8. Select OK.

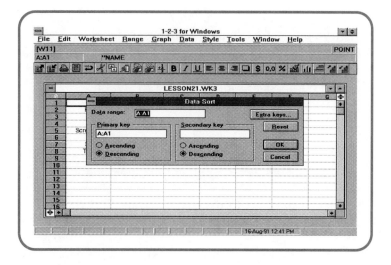

Figure 21.1 You specify sort keys in the Data Sort dialog box.

Field names in the sort range If you mistakenly include the field names in the sort range, they will be sorted like any other record. To recover, use the Edit Undo command.

When a database table is sorted, the sorted records are placed in the same worksheet range as the original table. No changes are made to data in the database; only the position of records in the table is changed.

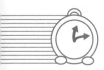

Saving the original order If you want to retain the original database record order as well as the new, sorted order, first copy the database table to a new worksheet location, then sort the copy.

116

Searching a Database

In this lesson, you'll learn how to find information in your database.

Searching for Information

When you have created a database, you'll often need to locate specific records. For example:

- In a mailing list database, find all addresses in New York.

- In a parts inventory database, find all parts with fewer than 5 on hand.

Searching a database for specific information is called a *query*. A query finds the records that meet one or more criteria. In the above examples, "STATE = NY" is a criterion, as is "Quantity on hand less than 5." To perform a query, you must specify exactly the criteria you are interested in.

Setting Up Criteria

The first step in searching for database information is setting up a criteria range. The criteria range contains information that tells 1-2-3 for Windows what you are searching for. A criteria range has the following characteristics:

- It contains as many columns as there are database fields being searched.

- It contains at least 2 rows.

- It contains the names of the fields being searched in the first row.

- It contains search criteria in the second and additional rows.

Figure 22.1 shows a sample database table and a criteria range containing field names and one criteria. Note that the criteria range need not contain all of the table's field names (although it does no harm), but only the names of the fields being searched.

To find an exact match for a label or value field, enter the criterion in the cell directly under the field name in the criteria range. For example, the criteria range:

QOH
5

would match all records where the QOH field contains the value 5. Likewise, the criteria range:

NAME
Hammer

would match all records where the NAME field contains the label "Hammer." 1-2-3 for Windows normally does not distinguish between upper- and lowercase letters, so "Hammer" will match "HAMMER," "hammer," and so on. Label prefix characters are ignored in queries.

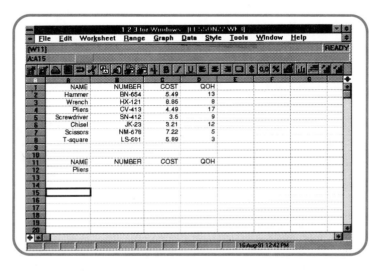

Figure 22.1 The range A11..D12 is a criteria range.

A criterion can contain the following relational operators:

Symbol	Meaning
=	equal to
<> or ~	not equal to
>	greater than
<	less than
<=	less than or equal to
>=	greater than or equal to

When applied to values, these operators have their usual meanings. For example, the criterion:

QOH
<5

will match all records where the QOH field contains a value less than 5. When applied to labels, the relation operators refer to alphabetical order. Thus, the criterion:

NAME
<B

The preceding discussion is only an introduction to 1-2-3 for Windows criteria ranges. See your 1-2-3 for Windows documentation for more information.

Data Query Operations

Once you have set up your criteria range, there are several different query commands available. These commands are accessed via the Data Query command, which displays the Data Query dialog box, shown in Figure 22.2.

The text boxes in this dialog box are used as follows:

Input range specifies the range containing the database table to be queried. The first row of the input range must contain the database table's field names.

Criteria range specifies the criteria range (as explained earlier in this lesson).

Output range specifies where the results of the query operation are to be placed. An output range is needed only for some query operations.

The buttons in the Data Query dialog box select the specific query operation to perform. This section covers the three most important query commands.

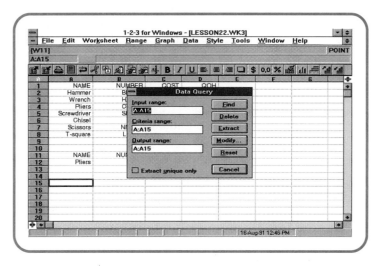

Figure 22.2 The Data Query dialog box.

Data Query Find

Use Data Query Find to locate records for viewing or modification. When you select Find, 1-2-3 highlights the first record in the input range that matches the criteria. You can then use the following keys:

Keys	Action
Left and right arrows	Move between fields in the current record.
Up and down arrows	Move to the previous or next matching record.

121

Enter or Esc	Returns you to the Data Query dialog box.
F2 (EDIT)	Edit the current cell.
Home or End	Move to the first or last matching record in the database table.
F7 (Query)	Ends the Data Query Find operation.

To find information in a database table:

1. Set up a criteria range, as described earlier in this lesson, that will match the information you are looking for.

2. Select Data Query to display the Data Query dialog box (Figure 22.2).

3. In the Input range text box enter the address or range names of your data table. This range should include all records plus the row of field names at the top of the table.

4. In the Criteria range text box enter the address or range name of your criteria range.

5. Select Find. The first matching record is highlighted, and you can move around using the keys as described previously.

Data Query Extract

Use Data Query Extract to copy matching records from the input range to the output range. All records that match the criteria are copied, including cell attributes. The input range is not modified. If the input range contains formulas, the results of the formulas are copied, not the formulas themselves.

The *output range* is a single row containing the database field names. 1-2-3 for Windows will place extracted records in the rows below the output range. Any existing data in this region will be overwritten.

To extract specific records from a database table:

1. Set up a criteria range, as described earlier in this lesson, that will match the records you want to extract.

2. Select Data Query to display the Data Query dialog box (Figure 22.2).

3. In the Input range text box, enter the address or range name of your data table. This range should include all records plus the row of field names at the top of the table.

4. In the Criteria range text box, enter the address or range name of your criteria range.

5. In the Output range text box, enter the address of the range you want the records extracted to.

6. Select Extract. All matching records in the database table are copied to the output range.

Data Query Delete

Use the Data Query Delete command to delete matching records from the database table. Before using Delete, it is a good idea to use Data Query Find to examine the matching records to verify that you will delete the proper ones. 1-2-3 for Windows deletes matching records from the database table and moves remaining records up to fill the blank rows.

Undoing a Deletion A Data Query Delete operation can be reversed with the UNDO command.

In this lesson, you learned how to query a database table for specific information.

This is the final lesson in the *10 Minute Guide to 1-2-3 for Windows*. You now should know enough about the program to start using it for real-world tasks. Future "lessons" will come as you use 1-2-3 for Windows and become more and more familiar with its features.

Overtime

Table of Functions

Following are the most commonly used @functions.

Statistical Functions

@function	Value returned or action	Example
@COUNT	The number of nonblank cells in a range.	@COUNT(A1..A100) Returns the number of nonblank cells in the range A1..A100.
@MAX	The maximum value in a range.	@MAX(SALES) Returns the largest value in any cell in the named range SALES.
@MIN	The minimum value in a range.	@MIN(SALES) Returns the smallest value in any cell in the named range SALES.
@AVG	The arithmetic average of values in a range.	@AVG(SALES) Returns the average of all values in the named range SALES.

@function	Value returned or action	Example
@STD	The standard deviation of values in a range.	@STD(B1..B20) Returns the standard deviation of the values in the range B1..B20.
@SUM	The sum of values in a range.	@SUM(B1..B20) Returns the sum of all values in the range B1..B20.

Mathematical and Trigonometric Functions

@function	*Value returned or action*	*Example*
@@ABS	The absolute (positive) value of a value.	@ABS(A1) Returns the value in cell A1 converted to a positive value.
@LN	The natural logarithm of a value.	@LN(B20) Returns the natural logarithm of the value in cell B20.
@SQRT	The square root of a value.	@SQRT(D6) The square root of the value in cell D6.
@SIN	The sine of an angle.	@SIN(A5) The sine of the angle in cell A5.
@RAND	A random number.	@RAND Returns a random number between 0 and 1.

@function	Value returned or action	*Example*
@ROUND	Rounds a value to a specified number of decimal places.	@ROUND(1.45612,2) Returns the value 1.45612 rounded to 2 decimal places (i.e., 1.46).

Financial Functions

@function @function	Value returned or action	*Example*
@PMT	The periodic payment on a loan with given amount, interest rate, and term.	@PMT(2000, .1/12, 36) Returns the monthly payment on a 36 month loan at 10% annual interest.
@IRR	The internal rate of return for a series of cash flows.	@IRR(0.1,A1..A50) Returns the internal rate of return for the cash flow values in the range A1..A50, with an initial guess of 10%.
@FV	The future value of a series of equal payments.	@FV(100, .1/12, 120) Returns the total amount you will have if you invest $100 per month for 10 years (120 months) in an account that pays 10% annual interest.

Logical Functions

@function	Value returned or action	Example
@EXACT	Compares two strings and determines if they are identical.	@EXACT(A1, A2) Returns 1 if the strings in cells A1 and A2 are identical; returns 0 if they are not identical.
@IF	Evaluates a condition and determines if it is true.	@IF(A1 > A2) Returns 1 if the value in cell A1 is greater than the value in cell A2; returns 0 otherwise.

String Functions

@function	Value returned or action	Example
@UPPER	A string converted to upper case.	@UPPER(A1) Returns the label in cell A1 with all letters converted to uppercase.
@LOWER	A string converted to lower case.	@LOWER(A1) Returns the label in cell A1 with all letters converted to lowercase.
@LENGTH	The number of characters in a string.	@LENGTH(A1) Returns the number of characters in the label in cell A1.

@function	Value returned or action	Example
@RIGHT	A specified number of characters from the right end of a string.	@RIGHT(A1, 5) Returns the last 5 characters in the label in cell A1.

Special Functions

@function	Value returned or action	Example
@ROWS	The number of rows in a range.	@ROWS(SALES) Returns the number of rows in the named range SALES.
@COLS	The number of columns in a range.	@COLS(SALES) Returns the number of columns in the named range SALES.
@INFO	Information about the current 1-2-3 session.	@INFO("memavail") Returns the amount of memory currently available.

Date and Time Functions

@function	Value returned or action	Example
@TIME	The time serial number for a specified time.	@TIME(6,30,0) Returns the time serial number corresponding to 6:30AM.

@function	Value returned or action	Example
@TODAY	The date serial number corresponding the today's date.	@TODAY Returns the date serial number corresponding to the date set on the computer's system clock.
@DATE	The date serial number for a given date.	@DATE(91,12,25) Returns the date serial number for December 25, 1991.
@YEAR	The year of a date serial number.	@YEAR(A1) Returns the year of the date serial number in cell A1.

DOS and Windows Primer

This section highlights some of the DOS and Windows procedures you will use during your work with this program.

DOS is your computer's Disk Operating System. It functions as a go-between program that lets the various components of your computer system talk with one another. Whenever you type anything using your keyboard, whenever you save data on a disk, whenever you print a file, DOS interprets the commands and coordinates the task.

Windows is an operating environment that works with DOS. Windows sits on top of DOS and provides a user-friendly interface to some of DOS's more complicated procedures. Just as DOS functions as a go-between for the components of your computer system, Windows functions as a go-between for you and DOS.

The following pages explain how to run some essential DOS functions on your computer, as well as how to use Windows to perform more advanced tasks.

Using DOS

If you are running Windows, your computer has a hard disk. DOS is probably already installed on your hard disk, which means that when you turn on your computer, DOS automatically loads itself without any special installation. (Some computer manufacturers configure their computers so that Windows also automatically loads when you turn on your PC. If this is the case, you might want to skip the next section.)

Once DOS is loaded, you should see a prompt (known as the DOS prompt) on your screen that looks something like **C:** or **C:>**. This prompt tells you which disk drive is currently active; most hard drives are labeled as drive C. The diskette drives located on the front of your computer are drives A and B. If you only have one diskette drive, it's the A drive. If you have two diskette drives, the top or left drive is usually A, and the bottom or right drive is B.

You can change to a different drive at any time by following these steps:

1. If you're changing to a diskette drive, make sure that there is a formatted disk in that drive.

2. Type the letter of the drive you wish to change to, followed by a colon. For example, type **A:**.

3. Press Enter. The DOS prompt changes to show that the drive you selected is now the active drive.

Managing Directories and Files in DOS

Because hard disks hold much more information than diskettes, hard disks are often divided into smaller parts, called *directories*. Each directory is like a branch off the main tree trunk; in the computer world, the main tree trunk is called the *root directory*. Each directory branching from the root directory can branch out to other *subdirectories*;

each subdirectory can also have branching subdirectories, and so on. Note that each directory and subdirectory has a unique name that allows you to access that directory from DOS or Windows.

Making Directories in DOS

To create a new directory use the DOS Make Directory command. This command is invoked when you type MD, followed by the name of the new directory (including the complete path). For example, to create a directory called NEW, you would type:

MD C:\NEW

If you wanted to create a subdirectory called NEW-A as a branch from the NEW directory, you would type:

MD C:\NEW\NEW-A

Changing Directories in DOS

To change to a different directory, use the Change Directory command. This command is invoked when you type CD, followed by a backslash (\) and the name of the directory you wish to change to. For example, to move to the NEW directory, you would type:

CD \NEW

If you wanted to move to the NEW-A subdirectory that branches from the NEW directory, you would type the complete path in the Change Directory command, as follows:

CD \NEW\NEW-A

Listing Files with DOS

To display files within a directory, use the DOS Directory command. Follow these steps:

1. Type **CD** command to change to the directory.

2. Type **DIR**.

3. Press Enter.

DOS displays a list of files in this directory.

Copying Files with DOS

The DOS Copy command copies the selected file to a second location, either on your hard disk or on a diskette. Follow these steps to copy a file:

1. Use the CD command to move to the directory that contains the source file.

2. Type the command line:

     COPY *filename1 filename2*

   where *filename1* is your original file and *filename2* is the new file. You can also specify a new path for the target file, using the syntax *[drive]:\[path]\filename2*.

3. Press Enter.

DOS then copies the file.

Deleting Files with DOS

DOS uses the Erase command to delete files from your disks. To delete a file, follow these steps:

1. Use the CD command to move to the directory.

2. Type the command line:

   ERASE *filename*

3. Press Enter.

4. When DOS asks for confirmation, press Y.

DOS then deletes the file.

Using DISKCOPY to Make Backups of the 1-2-3 for Windows Program Disks

Before you install 1-2-3 for Windows on your hard disk, you should make *backup copies* of the original program disks. By using these backup copies to install the program, you avoid the risk of damaging the original disks.

Obtain several blank 5.25" or 3.5" disks. You'll need the same number and type of disks as the disks from your 1-2-3 for Windows package. The type of disk should be marked on the package. There's no need to format the disks because the DISKCOPY command will do this automatically if necessary. DISKCOPY differs from the normal COPY command in that it copies the contents of an entire disk. Follow these steps:

1. Change to drive C by typing C: and pressing Enter.

2. If the DISKCOPY program file is in a separate directory, change to that directory by typing cd*(name of directory)*. For example, if the file is in the C:\DOS directory, type CD \DOS at the C: prompt, and press Enter.

3. Type DISKCOPY A: A: or DISKCOPY B: B:, depending on which drive you're using to make the copies, then press Enter. A message appears, telling you to insert the source diskette into the diskette drive.

4. Insert the original 1-2-3 for Windows disk you want to copy (the *source diskette*) into drive A (or B) and press Enter. DOS copies the disk into memory, then displays an on-screen message telling you to insert the *target diskette* (one of your blank disks) into the diskette drive.

5. Remove the source diskette, insert one of your blank diskettes into the drive, and press Enter. DOS copies the files from memory onto the blank disk, formatting it if necessary. DISKCOPY may prompt you to swap the target and source disk one or more times.

6. When the copying is complete, a message appears asking if you want to copy another diskette. Remove the target disk from the drive and label it with the same title and number that appears on the original source disk.

7. If you have another diskette to copy, press Y and return to step 4. Repeat this procedure for all the original 1-2-3 for Windows diskettes; remember to label each target diskette to match the corresponding source diskette.

8. When you have finished copying the last disk, answer N when DOS asks you if you want to copy another disk.

Remember to put the original disks back into their box and to store them in a safe place.

Basic Windows Procedures

Windows is a Graphical User Interface (GUI) for DOS-based computers. Many users consider the Windows screen (interface) friendlier than the DOS prompt. Windows includes a program called the File Manager that allows you to work with disks, directories, and files. To properly use Windows, however, you have to master some techniques that might be unfamiliar to a typical DOS user.

Starting Windows

To start Windows, follow these steps:

1. Change to the drive that contains your Windows files, usually drive C:.

2. Change to the directory that contains your Windows files, usually C:\WINDOWS, by typing:

   CD \WINDOWS.

3. Type WIN and press Enter. Windows will start and display its opening screen, the Program Manager.

Using the Mouse

One Windows procedure that might be new to a DOS user is the use of the mouse. Mastering the mouse is essential to effective Windows performance. Here are the basic mouse procedures you need to know:

Action	**Result**
Point	Move the mouse pointer to an item on-screen.
Click	Press and release the left mouse button once (quickly); often used to highlight an item in Windows.
Double-click	Press and release the left mouse button twice (quickly); often used to select an item in Windows.
Drag	Press the mouse button and hold it down while you move the mouse; this enables you to grab an on-screen object and move it across the screen.

While the mouse is recommended for most efficient Windows use, you can use the keyboard for many of the same operations. In many cases, Windows and Windows applications let you use special function key and combination key shortcuts to quickly access menu items and commands via the keyboard.

Managing Directories and Files with the Windows File Manager

Windows includes a special program called the File Manager. The File Manager simplifies many of the file-related tasks traditionally implemented by DOS commands, including working with directories, formatting disks, and listing, copying, and deleting files. Most users find it easier to work with the icons and menus of the Windows File Manager than trying to remember the exact syntax needed to use traditional DOS commands. To open the File Manager, double-click on the File Manager icon in the Main Program Group.

Making Directories with the File Manager

The File Manager displays both a visual representation of your directory tree and a list of individual files in each directory. When the File Manager first starts, you are shown a tree with all the main directories branching off from the root directory of your current disk drive. You can change drives displayed by clicking on the appropriate drive icon.

To make a new directory, follow these steps:

1. Pull down the File menu.

2. Select the Create Directory option.

3. Type the path and name of the new directory in the dialog box.

4. Close the dialog box by clicking on the OK button or by pressing Enter.

Changing Directories with the File Manager

The File Manager displays a tree listing all directories branching off from the root directory. You can display subdirectories by clicking on any directory icon that shows a plus (+) sign. You can make any directory or subdirectory active by moving the mouse pointer to the directory name and clicking the mouse button. The active directory name is now highlighted.

Listing Files with the File Manager

To display the contents of any directory, follow these steps:

1. Highlight the appropriate directory or subdirectory.

2. Double-click on the directory icon.

   Windows displays a directory window that lists all the files in the selected directory. You can display multiple directory windows on-screen simultaneously.

Copying Files with the File Manager

Copying files from one directory to another or from one disk to another is easy with Windows. To copy a file, follow these steps:

1. Select the file to copy in the directory window by placing the mouse pointer over the file name and

clicking the mouse button. The file name is now highlighted.

2. To copy the file to another directory, click and hold the left mouse button over the highlighted file, and then drag the file out of the directory window to the appropriate directory in the directory tree. (When you drag the file, the mouse pointer changes to a small file icon.)

3. With the mouse pointer positioned over the target directory, release the mouse button to drop the copy of the file into the directory.

You can also copy the file to another disk by dropping the file icon onto one of the drive icons at the top of the directory file window. Make sure that if the target drive is a floppy drive, it contains a formatted floppy disk.

Deleting Files with the File Manager

To delete a file with the File Manager, follow these steps:

1. Select the file to delete in the directory window.

2. Pull down the File menu.

3. Click on the Delete option.

4. When the dialog box appears, click on the Delete button to delete the highlighted file, or on the Cancel button to cancel the delete operation.

Index

D